Living in Style

A Guide to Historic Decoration and Ornament

Oliver Garnett

THE NATIONAL TRUST

For Molly and Jenny

First published in 2002 by
National Trust Enterprises Ltd
36 Queen Anne's Gate, London SW1H 9AS
www.nationaltrust.org.uk/bookshop

Text copyright © The National Trust 2002

No part of this publication may be reproduced in any material form whether by photocopying or storing in any medium by electronic means whether or not transiently or incidentally to some other use for this publication without the prior written consent of the copyright owner, except in accordance with the provisions of the Copyright, Designs and Patents Act 1988 or under the terms of the licence issued by the Licensing Agency Limited of 33–34 Alfred Place, London WC1.

Cataloguing in Publication Data is available from the British Library

ISBN 0 7078 0313 6

Designed and typeset by
Sarah Mattinson: www.truedesign.co.uk

Picture Research by
Oliver Garnett and Helen Dunkerley

Index by T. D. K. Pearce

Colour reproduction by Acculith 76, Barnet

Printed and bound in Italy by
G. Canale & C. S.p.A

endpapers: **A Gothic Revival wallpaper at Oxburgh Hall in Norfolk.**
p.1: **A Green Man in the Elizabethan plasterwork of the Long Gallery at Powis Castle in Powys.**
pp.2–3: **A Robert Adam door-handle at Saltram in Devon.**
pp.8–9: **A seventeenth-century 'flamestitch' hanging in the Fettiplace Closet at Chastleton House in Oxfordshire.**
pp.40–41: **A late eighteenth-century plasterwork frieze by Michael Stapleton in the Drawing Room at Ardress, Co. Armagh.**
pp.72–3: **An Elizabethan needlework long cushion decorated with oak leaves at Hardwick Hall in Derbyshire.**

Cover, featuring NTPL images used inside the book photographed by *(front panel, top row from left to right)*: Andreas von Einsiedel, John Hammond, Andreas von Einsiedel, John Hammond; *(second row)* both by John Hammond; *(third row, left to right)*: Michael Caldwell, Ian Shaw, Geoffrey Frosh, National Trust/Waddesdon Manor (photo: Hugo Maertens); *(bottom row, left to right)*: Andreas von Einsiedel (two pictures); James Mortimer, John Hammond. *(back panel, third picture on third row)* Andreas von Einsiedel.

Contents

Introduction
6   Seeing Patterns

**Chapter One:
Questions of Style**

10   What is Style?
12   Not What it Seems
14   Mixing Styles
18   Style and Status
22   Consuming Style: London
24   Consuming Style: The Grand Tour
26   Transmitting Style: The Sixteenth Century
28   Transmitting Style: The Seventeenth and Eighteenth Centuries
30   Transmitting Style: The Nineteenth Century
32   Revivalism
34   The Period Room
38   Country House Style

**Chapter Two:
Components of Style**

42   The Classical Orders
44   Doric
46   Ionic
48   Corinthian
50   Tuscan
51   Composite
52   Acanthus
54   Anthemion
56   Arabesque
58   Cartouche
59   Griffin
60   Grotesque
62   Guilloche
64   Strapwork
66   Swag
68   Trophy
70   Vitruvian Scroll

Chapter Three: Historical Styles and Designers

74   Renaissance
76   Tudor
78   Elizabethan
80   Jacobean
82   Caroline
84   Baroque
86   Restoration
88   Louis XIV Style
90   André-Charles Boulle (1642–1732)
92   William and Mary
94   Daniel Marot (c.1663–1752)
96   Queen Anne
98   Georgian
100 Palladianism
102 William Kent (1685–1748)
104 Gothick
106 Rococo
110 Louis XV Style
114 Chinoiserie
118 Thomas Chippendale (1718–79)
120 Neo-classicism
124 Robert Adam (1728–92)
128 Louis XVI Style
130 Greek Revival
132 Pompeian
134 Etruscan
136 Regency
140 Egyptian Revival
142 Rococo Revival
144 Norman Revival
146 Indian Style
148 Victorian
152 Gothic Revival
154 A.W.N. Pugin (1812–52)
156 William Burges (1827–81)
158 Crace Family
160 Renaissance Revival
162 Jacobethan
164 William Morris (1834–96)
166 Arts and Crafts
170 Aesthetic
174 Art Nouveau
176 Edwardian
178 Art Deco
180 Modern Movement
182 John Fowler (1906–77)

184 Bibliography
188 Index
192 Picture Credits and Acknowledgements

Seeing Patterns

In July 2001 the archive of the Lyons silk-weaving firm of Bianchini Férier was auctioned at Christie's in London. Laid out on long trestle tables were hundreds of pattern-books and portfolios, containing thousands of scraps of fabric and sheets of original designs. Between 1912 and about 1928 the artist Raoul Dufy produced over 4,000 different designs for Bianchini Férier fabrics. Dufy was only one designer working for one company, and he worked largely in one style – Art Deco (see p.178). Yet this book attempts to look at styles from the Renaissance to the Modern Movement. How on earth can one find one's way through such a profusion of pattern?

I have approached the problem from three directions. The first section of this book discusses some of the broader issues concerning style: how, for instance, it has been perceived, consumed, transmitted and revived. In the second section, which is arranged alphabetically, I briefly define some of the key terms used to describe ornament and the other components of style. In the third section, which is arranged chronologically, I provide thumbnail sketches of the major historical style labels used in Britain over the last 500 years and of designers who have been so influential in Britain that they have themselves become labels for styles. I have limited myself to terms in common use and not attempted to invent new ones, as Osbert Lancaster did in *Homes Sweet Homes* (which remains the most amusing, and the best, book on the subject).

As I hope will become apparent, there are many common threads, which offer a path through the maze of different patterns.

Because this is a National Trust book, I have taken my examples largely from National Trust properties that are regularly open to the public. I have also concentrated on style and ornament as they are represented in domestic interiors in England, Wales and Northern Ireland and deliberately said little about style in external architecture and garden design. This makes the task more manageable, but it inevitably introduces distortions: most obviously, the focus is on the rural elite during the 'long eighteenth century' (1660–1830); the styles of working- and middle-class urban interiors are poorly represented.

The art historian E.H. Gombrich warned: 'We must never forget that style, like any other uniform, is also a mask which hides as much as it reveals.' The labels used to define particular historical styles are even more slippery creatures. Many have been attached to a style in retrospect, long after its creative energy has expired. Those named after monarchs rarely coincide with their reigns or reflect their personal tastes. Many styles are easier to illustrate visually than to define – hence the density of pictures in this book.

There are many common threads, which offer a path through the maze of different patterns

Yet if one is to describe anything with words, verbal labels are unavoidable, and many of those included here have been in use for centuries. If you are to get the most enjoyment and understanding out of a visit to any historic house, it helps if you are able to decipher 'the language of style'. Explaining that language's vocabulary and grammar – in words and images – is the purpose of this book.

left: **Raoul Dufy designed the 'Les Arums' printed fabric that once furnished Lady Dorothy D'Oyly Carte's Bedroom at Coleton Fishacre in Devon.**
right: **A pattern-book from the Bianchini Férier archive.**

1: Questions of Style

above: **The Uppark doll's house of *c*.1735–40 opens to reveal a miniature, but minutely detailed, replica of a Palladian interior of that period.**

What is Style?

What is style? The *Oxford English Dictionary* provides no fewer than 28 definitions of the word. The one we want is number 21a:

A particular mode or form of skilled construction, execution, or production; the manner in which a work of art is executed, regarded as characteristic of the individual artist, or of his time and place.

As the first part of this definition proposes, the historical styles described in Chapter Three demanded skill from those who conceived and executed them – in most cases, a very high level of skill. In this sense, they are manifestations of 'high style', the product of a cultural elite who had the leisure, money and imagination to spend on transforming their appearance and surroundings as they wished. At this level, style implied choice, but it was a choice constrained by social pressures both to conform and to compete (see p.18). The choice of possible styles became increasingly and bewilderingly wide from the late eighteenth century, the moment when historians first began seriously to analyse and identify visual styles.

Individual styles can be identified by particular external markers – what might be called the Sherlock Holmes method: 'You mentioned your name as if I should recognise it, but beyond the obvious facts that you are a bachelor, a solicitor, a Freemason and an asthmatic, I know nothing whatever about you.' Thus the C-scroll signals Rococo, and the pointed arch, Gothic. Many more such markers are described and illustrated in these pages.

But style does not simply describe. It also judges. Many style labels, such as Rococo, began as terms of abuse, and the pursuit of 'fashionability' required a continually changing critique of the current style. Some even questioned the consequences of this pursuit. After the critic John Ruskin had stayed in a fashionable but visually dreary and uncomfortable seaside hotel in Scarborough in 1877, he concluded gloomily: 'This is what the modern British public thinks is "living in style".' A constant theme of this book is the British debt to designers and design ideas from overseas, which some have ascribed to the state's lack of support for skilled native craftsmen and sympathetic designers. By contrast, in the eighteenth century France dominated the market for luxury furniture and textiles because of the power of the royal workshops.

Style naturally encourages one to make connections. The German philosopher Georg Hegel proposed a *Zeitgeist*, or 'spirit of the age', which he believed linked all the cultural manifestations of a particular era or place. This notion has obvious relevance for the study of style. It was accepted by many artists and cultural historians and might seem to explain the rapid international spread of phenomena such as Neo-classicism. Many designers, such as Daniel Marot and Robert Adam, also took a similarly holistic approach in conceiving their interior décors. But the idea needs to be used with care, as styles can be mixed (see p.14), and it becomes particularly difficult to maintain from the early nineteenth century onwards, when more and more different styles were being revived at the same moment (see p.148). Many designers, such as William Morris, made significant contributions precisely because they seemed to be reacting *against* prevailing fashion (although Hegel would have argued that it was from this very process of conflict that the *Zeitgeist* was forged). It is perhaps easier to establish date and locality for vernacular architecture and furniture of the kind that Morris loved, because they were less susceptible to rapidly changing fashion and less influenced by foreign styles.

Today, the very idea of style has got a bad name. The word has been worn out by overuse, to the extent that 'Georgian-style' now means 'not Georgian'. A recent Argos catalogue advertises as 'Jacobean' an 'oak effect' bookcase with 'leaded effect glass doors' and 'antique brass effect handles'. Things are not much better in the study of style. The old school of architectural history based on vague stylistic comparisons has been replaced by a much more scholarly method, which demands documentary evidence for attributions. At the same time, the new school of art history prefers the study of material culture and iconography to stylistic analysis. But the very fact that style is now considered old hat is implicit acknowledgement that the cycle of fashion has not been abolished. And in the era of the global brand, style still maintains its hold over us all.

Not What it Seems

The Great Hall at Baddesley Clinton in Warwickshire is dominated by an impressive stone chimneypiece. It was made for the house in the early 1600s, and the design of the bottom half is based on an engraving in Sebastiano Serlio's *The Five Books of Architecture*, which had been circulating in England since the 1570s. That much is clear. But if you compare the fireplace and the engraving more closely, it becomes apparent that the middle sections of the pilasters (attached columns) on either side have been put in upside-down. Indeed, the fireplace was first installed in the first-floor Great Parlour over the gatehouse and moved to the Great Hall only in 1752, when the mistake must have happened. This is just one illustration of how important it is to look critically at the decoration of any historic interior.

Tap many a solid-looking marble column in a country house, and, as often as not, it will ring hollow. This is because it is made of scagliola – gypsum plaster bound in glue and coloured with pigment, which, when dried and polished, is almost indistinguishable from marble. Similar tricks can be played more cheaply with paint. Indeed, in the seventeenth, early eighteenth and nineteenth centuries any high-quality house-painter had to be able to imitate the various kinds of marble and wood, bronze, mother-of-pearl, tortoise-shell, leather and even damask. So, for instance, in the 1660s Sir Roger Pratt specified the following for the house he was building at Kingston Lacy in Dorset: 'Painting plain, veined, grained. Imitation either of marble of some sorts, or of cedar, walnut, princeswood etc. all blues, greens, yellows and such like.' Until quite recently the panelled Balcony Room at Dyrham

left: **The shaded section of this engraving in Serlio's *Five Books of Architecture*** provided the source for a fireplace at Baddesley Clinton (opposite).

opposite: **When this fireplace was moved down to the Great Hall, the masons reassembled the upright sections the wrong way up.**

Tap many a solid-looking marble column in a country house, and, as often as not, it will ring hollow

Park in Gloucestershire was thought to be a rare surviving example of just such seventeenth-century decorative graining. It now turns out to be nineteenth century, but the original, even more unusual scheme survives beneath: the pilasters, entablature and mouldings were painted to resemble dark purple porphyry, while the panels imitate pinky-orange marble, and the skirting, grey stone.

The Dyrham scheme was painted in 1694 by Mark Anthony Hauduroy, who was probably a French craftsman. According to the leading nineteenth-century decorative painter John Gregory Crace (see p.158), it was also French craftsmen working for the Prince of Wales at Carlton House in London in the 1780s (see p.136) who reintroduced the fashion for marbling to Britain after it had fallen out of favour earlier in the century. Neo-classical decorators were also inspired by the discoveries of classical schemes of marbling in the excavated rooms at Pompeii and at the Villa Negroni in Rome, which Crace's son was to replicate at Ickworth in Suffolk in 1879 (illustrated on p.132).

By contrast, marbled paper never went out of fashion. It was first made in China in the tenth century but was not manufactured in Britain until the seventeenth century, when it became very popular for decorating the endpapers of books. But it was also used for covering boxes and for lining drawers, as in Chippendale's clothes press of 1767 at Nostell Priory in Yorkshire.

14 Questions of Style

right: **This group of mainly eighteenth-century porcelain at Charlecote Park, Warwickshire, once belonged to William Beckford (1760–1844). He happily mixed things of beauty in many styles to make Fonthill Abbey into a modern version of the Renaissance *Wunderkammern* he so admired. Exquisite curiosities in hard stones, shell and ivory sat beside Islamic metalwork, Japanese lacquer, Boulle furniture and Tudor Revival pieces. He also transformed his possessions by adding mounts in a different style. The Japanese crackle-glazed porcelain bottle on the left was mounted on a gilt-bronze stand decorated with a Greek Revival Vitruvian scroll and supported by lion's paw feet. The tall Chinese vase at the back also received Grecian handles to give it the shape of a Greek *krater* wine vase. The cobalt blue basin in the centre was turned into a miniature Roman bath by adding ormolu ring handles and a stand in the Louis XIV Revival style of the 1760s.**

Mixing Styles

It is rare to find a house built, decorated and furnished in a single style. Even when the owner was someone like Sir Nathaniel Curzon of Kedleston in Derbyshire, who in 1759 pulled down the existing house to build from scratch in the latest style, he brought old family treasures with him to furnish his new home. Curzon also retained the nearby Gothic church in which his ancestors were buried. Similarly, when Ernö Goldfinger had finished designing 2 Willow Road in London in the rationalist Modern Movement style, he found room in it not only for his own collection of anti-rationalist Surrealist pictures but also for his mother's ponderously nineteenth-century Austro-Hungarian furniture. Even, or perhaps especially, when the money is newly made, owners have wanted to surround themselves with antiques. So in the late nineteenth century the Rothschilds filled the Renaissance Revival Waddesdon Manor and the 'Old English' Ascott in Buckinghamshire with eighteenth-century French furniture and ceramics and eighteenth-century portraits by Reynolds and Gainsborough.

Over the years many old houses have been adapted and added to in a range of different styles. Saltram in Devon, for instance, has Palladian chimneypieces, Rococo plasterwork, Chinese wallpaper, Neo-classical decoration by Robert Adam, and a Regency porch. If you employ a designer with as fertile an imagination as Luke Lightfoot, you can achieve the same effect more quickly, as a visitor to Claydon House in Buckinghamshire in 1768 recorded in his diary: 'Lesser rooms … furnished in all tastes, as the Chinese Room, the Gothick Room, the French Room etc.'

Such stylistic diversity is most commonly found in garden buildings. Eighteenth-century Stourhead in Wiltshire boasted a Palladian Pantheon, a Gothic High Cross, a Chinese Umbrello and a Turkish Tent. By the mid-nineteenth century, when the choice of available styles was even more bewildering and events like the Great Exhibition of 1851 made a point of displaying the styles of all nations, the Batemans of Biddulph Grange in Staffordshire could happily juxtapose visions of China, Egypt, South America – and Cheshire. Indeed, the incongruity was part of the intended effect.

Occasionally, two styles are combined on the outside of a single house. Perhaps the most famous example is Castle Ward in Co. Down, which Bernard Ward rebuilt in the 1760s. The story goes that he favoured the Palladian style but that his wife Lady Anne wanted Gothick (the spelling here indicating the first phase of the Gothic Revival, from about 1740 to about 1780), and so they decided to have one façade of each. Mrs Delany, who visited in 1763, was dubious about the whole project: '*He* wants taste and *Lady Anne Ward*, his wife, is so whimsical that I doubt her judgement.' But there may

16 Questions of Style

above: **Lady Anne Ward's Gothick garden façade for Castle Ward.**
opposite: **Bernard Ward's Palladian entrance façade.**

'In the pictures of Claude ... we perpetually see a mixture of Grecian and Gothic employed with the happiest effect in the same building'

Richard Payne Knight, 1808

have been a serious point behind Lady Anne's choice. She was a descendant, through her mother, of James I and perhaps wanted to call to mind her distinguished Stuart ancestry through the choice of Gothic. Her family home, Cobham Hall in Kent, was also a mixture of styles: chiefly late Elizabethan, but with a classical centrepiece, added in 1661, possibly by John Webb. At Castle Ward the Gothick façade was essentially a veneer applied to a classically proportioned carcass, and it could not hide more fundamental disagreements. Ward and his wife parted not long after the house was finished.

It was much more acceptable to choose different styles for the public exterior and the private interior of a building. As Inigo Jones noted in the margin of his copy of Palladio's *Four Books of Architecture*: 'The outward ornaments ought to be solid, proportionable, according to the rules, masculine and inaffected. Where within the chimeras [mythical beasts, part-lion, goat and serpent] used by the ancients, the varied and composed ornaments, both of the house itself and the moveables within it are most commendable.' Hence the plain Palladian exteriors and the more delicate Rococo interiors of so many early eighteenth-century country houses. Hence, also, the sensible Arts and Crafts exterior of 1930s Coleton Fishacre in Devon conceals distinctly raffish Art Deco interiors.

Style and Status

Style has always reflected status. Indeed, advertising one's social position and wealth through lavish building and decoration has been justified as a form of civic duty for the upper ranks of society since at least the time of the Greek philosopher Aristotle, who argued that it was the responsibility of the wealthy man 'to furnish his house in a way suitable to his means, for that gives him a kind of distinction'. The Roman architectural writer Vitruvius encapsulated the idea in the Latin word *decor*, which Sir Henry Wotton defined in his *Elements of Architecture* (1624) as 'the keeping of a due Respect between the Inhabitant and the Habitation'. It is no accident that the words 'decorum' and 'decoration' come from the same root.

The social connotations of style are particularly complex in a hierarchical country like Britain, whose inhabitants are, as David Cannadine has noted, 'always thinking about who they are, what kind of society they belong to, and where they themselves belong in it'. In 1688 Gregory King divided English society into no fewer than 26 levels, and the peerage alone is conventionally divided into five ranks.

In the Middle Ages one of the most emphatic ways of establishing your social status was by receiving a 'licence to crenellate' from the Crown. This allowed you to build or rebuild your home with battlements. The ostensible purpose was purely practical – to fortify the building – and when Sir Edward Dalyngrigge was granted a licence to crenellate Bodiam in East Sussex in 1385, he claimed that his new castle would help to defend the country against the threat of French invasion. However, it seems almost certain that Bodiam's battlements were built for show rather than use, for they appear not just on the walls and towers but also on the chimneypieces and chimneypots, where they were meant purely as decoration that advertised Dalyngrigge's knightly status. For the same reason, crenellations also appear on the famous heraldic chimneypieces which are the principal surviving decoration in Ralph, Lord Cromwell's Tattershall Castle in Lincolnshire (built about 1440).

Heraldry was the most obvious and ubiquitous form of social advertisement. The right to bear a coat of arms was an important mark of gentility, sanctioned by the Crown and administered since 1484 by the College of Arms. If you are a nobleman, the form of coronet depicted indicates your exact position on the rungs of the peerage. A many-quartered coat of arms records an ancient lineage and distinguished marriage alliances. At Bodiam Dalyngrigge prominently displayed not only his own arms but also those of his heiress wife and his patron, Sir Robert Knollys.

During the sixteenth century the royal arms appear frequently in domestic interiors to demonstrate loyalty to the Crown and reinforce authority by association. Heraldry can feature in almost every kind of decoration – from floor coverings to ceiling bosses, from door-locks to picture frames, from stained-glass windows to enamelled drinking glasses. Because it was particularly associated with the Middle Ages, it was most commonly incorporated in Gothick and Gothic Revival decoration, but Renaissance and Neo-classical styles also made use of it.

Personal adornment sends obvious messages about the wearer and was subject to its own social code. During the sixteenth century the restrictions on what each class might wear became increasingly prescriptive, six sumptuary laws being passed between 1483 and 1539. In 1566 officials were posted at the gates of the City of London to make sure that everyone passing through them was dressed correctly for their rank.

In 1660, when the Crown, the traditional pinnacle of the English social hierarchy, was restored, the gentleman-architect Sir Roger Pratt wrote:

As there are three sorts of persons for whom houses are built of any consideration, viz. gentlemen, noblemen, and princes, so are there so many kinds of building which are to be formed according to the usual estates of men of such condition. [They differ] in either the costliness of the materials, the number of their ornament, or curiosity, in working them, or lastly in the spaciousness, and height of the whole building.

The French architect Jacques-François Blondel, writing in the 1770s, went a stage further, proposing that the client's rank should be 'the source from which the Architect determines the genre of his decoration'. He argued that the Ionic order was appropriate for clergymen, because it suggested temperance, and the Composite for judges, because it mixed moderation with delicacy; the Tuscan, on the other hand, was too rustic and humble for the town house of a nobleman. In practice, few architects in either France or Britain were so pedantic, and in the seventeenth and eighteenth centuries it is often quite difficult to distinguish the houses of the upper gentry from those of the aristocracy simply by their style. It is easier to separate the gentry house from that of lower classes: in Gloucestershire, for instance, one marker was the use of stone, rather than wooden, window mullions.

The status of individual rooms or suites of rooms within a country house also affected the extent and style of their decoration. In a late seventeenth-century and early eighteenth-century house it was the ceremonial 'rooms of parade' that were

'The boast of heraldry, the pomp of power, all that beauty, all that wealth e'er gave ...'

Thomas Gray, 1751

above: **One of Ralph, Lord Cromwell's heraldic chimneypieces at Tattershall Castle.**
opposite: **Like a car badge today, a coat of arms on a carriage door sent messages about the owner's status.**

decorated, with most money being devoted to the saloon, the main drawing room, the state bedroom (see p.94) and the principal staircase, particularly if it led up to a state dining room. The textiles chosen could be richly coloured, ornately worked and delicate because these rooms were usually shuttered and sheeted against light and dust and comparatively little used. By contrast, the family rooms, which were in constant use, were normally decorated with hard-wearing materials and sparely furnished with chairs covered in leather or wool rather than silk. So, for instance, at Houghton Hall in Norfolk the massive doors in the state apartment are made of solid mahogany, carved and gilded, whereas those in the family rooms are ungilded. The same distinction was drawn in eighteenth-century France, from where much of the luxury furnishings in such houses had originated. The grander *appartements de parade* were generally decorated with tapestries, antiques, Boulle furniture (see p.90), family portraits and paintings of historical and mythological subjects, whereas in the *appartements de société*, wallpapers, printed textiles and the lesser genres of painting were preferred. The choice of decorative subject-matter often reflected the function of the room: so, for instance, still-lifes of game and fruit were commonly hung in dining rooms, where the chimneypiece might be carved with bunches of grapes and the vine-wreathed head of Bacchus, god of wine, while scenes of passion appeared on bedroom ceilings. Perhaps the most bizarre example of this frequent practice is the frieze of billiard balls that runs around William Burges's billiard room at Knightshayes Court in Devon.

Hierarchy was an inextricable part of eighteenth-century English society, but so was ambition. What happened when someone refused to play by the rules and tried to step out of the class they were born into? The furniture-maker Thomas Sheraton suggested one answer in his *Cabinet Dictionary* (1803): 'When any gentleman is so vain and ambitious as to order the furnishings of his house in a style superior to his fortune and rank, it will be prudent in an upholsterer, by some gentle hints, to direct his choice to a more moderate plan.' But often 'gentle hints' did not work, and the nouveau-riche merchant, financier or lawyer who wants to become a country gentleman has been a recurring figure in British society since the sixteenth century. The most notorious were the nabobs, who returned to Britain in the 1760s with vast new fortunes made in India. Their wealth bred tall stories of the kind satirised in Mrs Bonhote's novel, *Ellen Woodley* (1790): 'One heard, that the bed in which Lady Alford slept, was decorated with a crescent of diamonds, and the curtains ornamented with festoons of pearls; – another, that the tables were solid gold, and the stoves silver.' Similar stories were told about the greatest of the nabobs, Robert Clive, conqueror of India, but they were equally fantastic. The house he built at Claremont in Surrey in 1771–4 was decorated with paintings celebrating his exploits but otherwise was in a restrained Neo-classical style.

As an increasingly wide range of decorative styles became available, so the choice you made could say much about your social position. Choosing Gothic was often a way of drawing attention to the ancient lineage of your family. By contrast, choosing classical implied that you had had a classical education or had made the Grand Tour of Italy (see p.24).

left: **The richly furnished Tapestry Room at Osterley Park formed the climax of an increasingly lavish suite of rooms.**

opposite: **A vine-wreathed head of Bacchus, god of wine, often decorated rooms meant for dining. This example is in the Little Parlour at Uppark.**

22 Questions of Style

above: **Wedgwood understood the value of royal endorsement. After Queen Charlotte had ordered a tea service in 1765, he renamed his creamware 'Queen's Ware' in her honour. This pair of creamware urns is at Saltram in Devon.**
right: **The ornate brass door-locks at Dyrham Park were made in Birmingham, but sold by a London locksmith.**
opposite: **The London trade card of William Parker, who designed spectacular cut-glass chandeliers for the new Assembly Rooms in Bath in 1771.**

Consuming Style: London

Special exhibitions turned shopping into an enjoyable spectacle

The highly competitive nature of eighteenth-century society not only challenged the traditional social hierarchy but also encouraged a consumer revolution that vastly increased the quantity of luxury goods in circulation and the market for them. Good taste was no longer the preserve of a tiny elite. The Rev. Nathaniel Forster summed up the position in 1767:

In England the several ranks of men slide into each other almost imperceptibly and a spirit of equality runs through every part of their constitution. Hence arises a strong emulation in all the several stations and conditions to vie with each other; and the perpetual ambition in each of the inferior ranks to raise themselves to the level of those immediately above them. In such a state as this fashion must have uncontrolled sway. And a fashionable luxury must spread through it like a contagion.

The luxury furnishings of the eighteenth-century country house were mostly acquired in London and the other rapidly expanding cities. As a great port, London received porcelain from China and fine furniture from France. It was also the centre of a thriving retail trade. So, for instance, the ornamental door-locks at Dyrham Park in Gloucestershire were made about 1694 by John Wilkes in Birmingham, the heart of British metalworking, but bought in London at Henry Walton's shop at 'the Sign of the Brass Lock and Key'.

Josiah Wedgwood, perhaps the most brilliant salesman of the eighteenth century, realised the importance of marketing his Staffordshire pottery through a London showroom in Great Newport Street, behind which was a decorating studio, where coats of arms and other final touches could be added. Special commissions, like the Green Frog Service for Catherine the Great, were promoted through exhibitions, part of a wider phenomenon that turned shopping into an enjoyable spectacle. In 1767 Wedgwood acknowledged 'the many good effects this must produce, when business & amusement can be made to go hand in hand'. As Horace Walpole noted in 1770: 'The rage to see these exhibitions is so great, that sometimes one cannot pass through the streets where they are.' Wedgwood advertised widely, cultivated 'Legislators of Taste' ('opinion-formers' in today's jargon) and kept a close eye on the increasingly rapid changes in fashion. When women started bleaching their hands artificially white in 1772, he saw it as an opportunity to sell them his contrasting black basaltes tea-ware.

Consuming Style: The Grand Tour

The rich could also afford to look beyond London for their luxuries. They could buy directly from the Continent via agents such as the dealer William Kent, who acquired Old Master paintings and casts of the most revered classical statues in Italy for Sir Nathaniel Curzon of Kedleston in 1758–60. Or they could buy in person, while making the Grand Tour.

In the eighteenth century the Grand Tour of Europe was supposed to set the

right: **George Lucy of Charlecote Park, painted by Pompeo Batoni in Rome in 1758.**
opposite: **The North Gallery at Petworth displays classical statuary bought in Italy in the mid-eighteenth century.**
below: **English *milordi* at play. A caricature by Thomas Patch at Dunham Massey.**

seal on a young gentleman's education. The programme usually included viewing the ruins of classical antiquity and the great art collections in the historic cities of Italy – Venice, Florence, Rome and Naples. But there were distractions. According to Horace Walpole, Sir Francis Dashwood of West Wycombe was 'seldom sober' during his entire time in Italy in 1739–40. Thomas Patch's caricatures of English *milordi* at play probably give an accurate picture of how they enjoyed themselves in the 1760s.

Nevertheless, there were still many travellers who brought home treasures from Italy to adorn their country homes. They might have their portrait painted by Batoni or Mengs wearing an embroidered waistcoat (both flowered silk and embroidery were cheap in Italy). Or they could pick up a souvenir of the places they had seen in the form of a micro-mosaic table or a Venetian view by Canaletto. Most collectors were happy to commission copies of the Renaissance and Baroque masters, because, until the French Revolution dispersed the Italian aristocratic collections, there were few really great old pictures to be bought and many opportunities to be duped. The Scottish artist and middleman William Patoun warned the young Earl of Exeter of the pitfalls about 1766: 'I need not caution your Lordship against purchases at Rome. You have too much taste to buy a bad thing and the good are not to be had. Jenkins an English Picture Dealer and Broker in the Caso will try to tempt you. He does not enjoy the best reputation in the World.' However, this does not seem to have stopped Patoun from encouraging Robert Clive to pay Jenkins £500 for a Tintoretto when Clive was on a holiday-cum-shopping expedition in Rome in 1773–4. Money was no object when it came to securing a Roman marble cat for his cat-loving wife, and he returned to Britain laden with Old Masters and classical statuary, some of which can be seen at Powis Castle.

Nathaniel Forster had likened the spread of luxury to a disease. It certainly offered no cure for Clive's growing depression, and only months after his return from Italy he committed suicide.

Transmitting Style: The Sixteenth Century

The transmission of styles was driven by the twin demands of display and consumption, but the whole process was hugely accelerated by the invention of printing in Europe in the 1440s.

Whereas previously design motifs had had to be carried in the head or laboriously copied by hand, they could now be duplicated easily, accurately and by the thousand.

During the sixteenth century, printing flourished most strongly in Antwerp, the

left: **The floral plasterwork of the Cartoon Gallery at Knole was probably based on Flemish engravings.**
opposite: **The stained glass in the Chapel at The Vyne was made by itinerant Flemish glaziers in the 1520s.**
below: **The panelling in the High Great Chamber at Hardwick Hall, which was probably made for the Old Hall in the 1580s, incorporates engravings of Roman emperors.**

Design motifs could now be duplicated easily, accurately and by the thousand financial and commercial heart of northern Europe. Here, the business of printing text and images became increasingly industrialised and sophisticated, being divided among specialist designers, engravers and publishers. Antwerp publishers such as Hieronymous Cock became famous for the quality and quantity of the ornament prints that they produced and distributed across the whole of Europe. Initially issued as single sheets, from the 1520s these prints were often bound up into pattern-books, intended for professional designers needing ideas for wood-carving, plasterwork, furniture, needlework, ceramics and metalwork – indeed, for every aspect of the well-to-do domestic interior.

Antwerp specialised in producing ornament prints that combined grotesque and strapwork decoration (see pp.60, 64). The pioneer of the genre was Cornelis Floris (1514–75), whose engravings of masks inspired a plasterwork frieze of the 1570s at Lyme Park in Cheshire and the carved overmantel in the Spangle Bedroom at Knole in Kent. The designs of Floris's disciple Hans Vredeman de Vries were even more widely copied in the decoration and furnishings of British houses. In the High Great Chamber at Hardwick Hall engravings were pasted directly on to the panelling.

When Henry Lyte of Lytes Cary in Somerset wanted to illustrate his 1578 translation of the herbal by the Flemish botanist Junius Dodoens, he simply reused engravings of plants that had been made in Antwerp; he also had his translation printed in Antwerp. It was engravings like these that were plundered for the floral motifs that appear on numerous Elizabethan and Jacobean plasterwork ceilings, such as those in the Cartoon Gallery at Knole and the Drawing Room at Gawthorpe Hall in Lancashire.

Antwerp exported its own design ideas and craftsmen and acted as a cultural exchange for the whole of Europe. In 1522 William Sandys, Henry VIII's Lord Chamberlain, brought over a team of ten Flemish glaziers, including the Antwerp-trained David Joris, who probably provided preparatory drawings for the stained glass in the Chapel at The Vyne in Hampshire. The rich ornament in the lower panels is Flemish in style but is also indebted to north Italian motifs, as transmitted by prints. The architectural setting is also Italian Renaissance in style. Similarly, the tiles now set into the Chapel floor were made in Flanders, but probably by Italian craftsmen, drawing on Italian coins and engravings. Itinerant Flemish wood-carvers may also have been responsible for the overmantels of the 1560s at Sizergh Castle in Cumbria. The patterns of several of the contemporary ribbed ceilings at Sizergh are based on engravings by the influential Italian architect Sebastiano Serlio, which were circulating widely as single sheets long before the first English translation of *The Five Books of Architecture* was published in 1611.

As Henry VIII's agent in Antwerp, the Tudor financier Sir Thomas Gresham served as an important link between that city and England. In the 1560s he was

inspired by the Antwerp stock exchange to erect the Royal Exchange in the heart of the City of London. He adopted the same style, using Flemish materials and a Flemish mason to build it and a Flemish engraver to record and publicise the result. Gresham went on to build himself a new house at Osterley in Middlesex. No record survives of the interior, but it was almost certainly decorated in a Flemish style. His tomb in Great St Helen, Bishopsgate, may well have been made in Antwerp; the carving on it was certainly based on a Floris ornament engraving. Gresham also left money to found Gresham College, London, to encourage the transmission of ideas in the same way that the Exchange had been designed to encourage the free flow of the capital on which the luxury trades depended.

Transmitting Style: The Seventeenth and Eighteenth Centuries

above: **A chimney-piece design from the fourth edition of William Pain's** The Practical Builder **(1787), one of his immensely successful pattern-books.**

opposite: **The grandly scrolled chimneypiece in the mid-eighteenth-century doll's house at Nostell Priory was based on a plate in James Gibbs's** A Book of Architecture **(1728).**

Few ornament prints were produced by British designers before the 1670s (one exception, by Edward Pierce, is illustrated on p.52). In response to the building boom triggered by the Great Fire of London in 1666, Robert Pricke began publishing suites of his own decorative engravings, but these were still largely copied from French and Italian examples, and Pricke continued to do a thriving trade retailing original continental prints. In 1694 Sir Christopher Wren noted English designers' continuing dependence on foreign ideas:

It was observed that our English artists are dull enough at inventions but when once a foreigne pattern is sett, they imitate soe well that commonly they exceed the originall.

One solution was for architects to publish their own designs. Colen Campbell started the trend with his *Vitruvius Britannicus* (1715, 1717, 1725), which included some of his own Palladian designs together with a puff for the new style, but most of the buildings included were in the Baroque style he was trying to supersede. More influential was William Kent's *Designs of Inigo Jones with some Additional Designs* (1727), which included Kent's own designs with details of doors and windows that were specifically intended for imitation (see p.102). In direct response to Kent, the following year James Gibbs published *A Book of Architecture*, the first volume to be devoted entirely to the work of a living British architect. Gibbs wanted it to be 'of use to such gentleman as might be concerned in Building, especially in the Country, where little or no assistance for Designs can be procured'. It offered illustrations 'of useful and convenient Buildings and proper Ornaments; which may be executed by any Workman who understands Lines'. Among those who made use of it was William Carew for his new house at Antony in remote Cornwall. It also provided the model for the White House in Washington.

Gibbs's book was a success, but, surprisingly, it was little imitated by later eighteenth-century architects, perhaps because such lavish volumes were expensive to produce. Much commoner were the more modest pattern-books – handy-sized collections of illustrations of details of doors, chimneypieces, windows, friezes and so on in a variety of styles. These served both as a visual aid for clients who might lack the technical vocabulary to describe what they wanted and as a reliable template for the craftsman.

Between 1758 and 1793 William Pain (*c*.1730–94?) published eleven such pattern-books, which were continually reprinted, making him, numerically speaking, the most popular eighteenth-century English author in America. Pain's *The Builder's Pocket Treasure* (1763) enabled the craftsman to 'have his whole Trade in his Pocket and not be at a loss for any Thing in the ordinary course of Profession'. His *Practical Builder* (1774) probably did more to disseminate the new Adam style than the architect's own publications (see p.124). Pain himself claimed:

The very great Revolution ... which of late has so generally prevailed in the decorative and ornamental department, will evince the necessity and eminent Utility of this publication.

By far the most important of all these eighteenth-century pattern-books was Thomas Chippendale's *The Gentleman's & Cabinet Maker's Director* (1754), which, despite being expensive (£1.14s for a bound copy of the first edition), was immensely influential in disseminating his designs for furniture. It also provoked competitors such as Thomas Johnson and Ince and Mayhew to go into print. (The particular styles Chippendale advocated are discussed on p.119.)

Pattern-books served as a visual aid for clients who might lack the technical vocabulary to describe what they wanted

30 Questions of Style

'How charming it would be if it were possible to cause these natural images to imprint themselves durably and remain fixed upon the paper!'

Henry Fox Talbot, 1833

above: **The Kitchen at Lindisfarne Castle photographed in 1910 for** Country Life **in the style of a seventeenth-century Dutch interior.**

right: **The drawing room at Clanna; Rebecca Dulcibella Orpen's first attempt at painting an interior. Such amateur efforts provide a vital colour record of nineteenth-century interior styles.**
opposite: **Several of Henry Fox Talbot's earliest photographs record the patterns of old lace. Photography has become the dominant medium for disseminating style.**

Transmitting Style: The Nineteenth Century

The architects' designs and pattern-books that transmitted stylistic ideas in the eighteenth century usually took the form of plans, elevations and decorative details. Perspective views of whole interiors by architects and designers were much rarer. In the early eighteenth century this deficiency was filled to some extent by portrait painters like the Devises, who travelled the country depicting gentry families in interior settings. But these family 'conversation-pieces' went out of fashion in the 1740s, and they are, in any case, often less revealing than the efforts of the amateur watercolourists (usually women), who increasingly from the late eighteenth century recorded the appearance of their own and their friends' surroundings in fascinating detail. Most of these amateur views remained pasted into private albums and so were of limited influence outside the immediate circle of family and friends, but the fashion was taken up by professionals, such as Nicholas Condy and Joseph Nash, both of whom published romantic watercolours of historic house interiors that encouraged the revival of Elizabethan and Jacobean styles in the mid-Victorian period (see p.162).

Photography has been the key medium for transmitting stylistic ideas ever since it was pioneered by Henry Fox Talbot at Lacock Abbey in Wiltshire in the 1830s. His earliest photographic images recorded flat patterns – the silhouettes of a fern frond and a piece of lace. The first surviving negative is of an architectural detail – an oriel window in the South Gallery at Lacock. Fox Talbot then went on to photograph a blurry, shadowy view of the South Gallery. Photography has developed in many ways since then, but these three categories of image remain central to the way decorative style is recorded and propagated.

A magazine like *Country Life*, which was founded by Edward Hudson in 1897, would have been inconceivable without photography; indeed, the magazine began life as *Country Life Illustrated*. The photographs published in its pages not only recorded the changing styles of British country houses over five centuries but also championed the way of life they depicted as still valid. When Hudson photographed his own holiday home at Lindisfarne Castle in 1910 for *Country Life*, Lutyens's work there was only four years old. Hudson's influential support for Lutyens also ensured that the architect's Arts and Crafts-based vision of country house style remained a potent force in the early twentieth century.

Photography disseminated the decorative styles of past and present as never before, but the real thing was also becoming increasingly available. Builders of country houses have always overreached themselves, but few did so as spectacularly as the 2nd Duke of Buckingham, who was forced to sell almost the entire contents of Stowe in Buckinghamshire in 1848 to meet his debts. The auction – perhaps the greatest of the nineteenth century – destroyed a spectacular decorative ensemble, but it also helped to furnish a hundred others across the world. Land sales from the Stowe estate also made it possible for the Rothschilds to settle in Buckinghamshire and create their own string of treasure houses.

Stowe was just the beginning. Historic collections were dispersed in growing numbers following the agricultural depression of the 1870s and the breaking of the entailment system, which had hitherto prevented the sale of family heirlooms. Auction houses and dealers were happy to handle contemporary as well as antique works of art. So, for instance, in the 1870s William Armstrong furnished Cragside in Northumberland with modern Victorian paintings bought almost entirely via the dealer Thomas Agnew from Christie's auction rooms. Through booms and depressions, the art market has continued to recycle style ever since.

Revivalism

In the world of style and ornament there is little that is absolutely original. Long before the Renaissance began reviving classical models in the fifteenth century, the remains of the ancient world were being quarried – metaphorically and literally – for ideas. Most of the styles described in this book are revivals of one kind or another (in some cases, even revivals of revivals). By the mid-Victorian period the proliferation of resurrected styles had reached epidemic proportions, to the despair of some critics. Sir Nikolaus Pevsner, one of the twentieth-century supporters of the Modern Movement, argued in 1961 that 'all reviving of styles of the past is a sign of weakness, because in revivals independent thinking and feeling matters less than the choice of patterns'. Horace Walpole saw it as a symptom of a broader political decline. In September 1778, when Britain was losing its grip on its American colonies, he wrote gloomily to William Cole:

Our empire is falling to pieces; we are relapsing to a little island. In that state, men are apt to imagine how great their ancestors have been, and when a kingdom is past doing anything; the few, that are studious, look into the memorials of past time; nations, like private persons, seek lustre from their progenitors when they have none in themselves.

Walpole was by then 61 years old and entitled to think that his world was going to the dogs. But as a young man, when the British Empire was at its eighteenth-century zenith, he was already showing a pioneering interest in 'the memorials of past time', particularly in the Gothic style, which he reinterpreted with a real creative flair when designing and furnishing his villa at Strawberry Hill (see p.104). Nor can the mass revivalism of the Victorian era really be seen as a sign of political decline. It perhaps reflects in part simply a wider knowledge of the styles created in other eras and by other civilisations. The real question is how well that knowledge is applied.

In *The Painter's Cabinet* (1828) T.H. Vanherman optimistically concluded: 'Taste … is to be acquired by gaining a competent knowledge of the old.' But for a revived style to be more than just a tasteful pastiche, it needs to be imaginatively rethought for its own time. When the 2nd Earl of Buckinghamshire began remodelling Jacobean Blickling Hall in Norfolk in the 1760s, he altered the circulation to suit modern needs by moving the old staircase into the Great Hall. He retained the pattern of the old Jacobean woodwork on the stairs but combined similar ornament with Neo-classical detail in the Peter the Great Room in an entirely new way.

'Gothic it was, and more Gothic it will be'
The 2nd Earl of Buckinghamshire on Blickling, 1765

opposite: **At The Vyne, Hampshire, John Chute's late eighteenth-century memorial to his most famous ancestor, the Civil War Speaker Chaloner Chute, is a highly sophisticated exercise in stylistic revivalism. The effigy recalls that for Thomas Sackville (d.1677) in Withyham church, Kent, and the sarcophagus on which he reclines is in the early seventeenth-century classical style of Inigo Jones. The stained-glass window is inspired by the work of another influential early seventeenth-century figure, Van Dyck.**

'Furnished with the rude comfort of the early times'

Joseph Nash, 1849

opposite: **King Charles's Room at Cotehele, where Charles I is supposed to have slept in September 1644. Like most of Cotehele, it has been preserved for showing to visitors, rather than living in, since the early nineteenth century.**
below: **The Stag Parlour at Lyme Park.**

The Period Room

Today, the term 'period room' is usually applied to the didactic re-creations of historic interiors found in places such as the Victoria & Albert Museum and the Geffrye Museum in London. It can, however, be traced back much further – to the country houses from which many of these interiors came. When we walk around a historic house, we may like to maintain the pretence that it enshrines untouched the style of one particular historical period, but in fact it often represents a later generation's imaginative reinterpretation of its past, intended for show rather than for day-to-day living.

Cotehele in Cornwall is a late medieval manor house hidden away in the upper reaches of the Tamar valley. In 1553 the Edgcumbes built themselves a new house across the river at Mount Edgcumbe, which from that date became their main residence. Despite this, they still respected their ancestral home. When Colonel Piers Edgcumbe gave Cotehele new windows in the mid-seventeenth century, he showed a regard for the building's ancient fabric that was unusual at this date by insisting that they copy the mouldings of the old. In the 1730s Sir Richard (later 1st Baron) Edgcumbe may have been responsible for hanging the late seventeenth-century Flemish tapestries that are still in the old rooms. This process was continued by his sons, Richard, who was part of the Gothick-fancying circle of Horace Walpole (see p.104), and George, who may have introduced the ebony chairs that were then thought to be Tudor. (They were, in fact, made in south-east India.) These dimly lit rooms were recorded by Nicholas Condy about 1840 in a series of atmospheric watercolours that make them seem immensely ancient, although the arrangement was then less than 100 years old. They have been little lived in or changed since.

There were many antiquarian-minded owners like the Edgcumbes who respected the ancient character of their homes, even when they decided to make major changes. In 1814 Thomas Legh of Lyme Park commissioned Lewis Wyatt to remodel the interiors, including the Little Parlour, a room with particular resonance for the family because the Jacobite 'Cheshire Gentlemen' had met there in the 1690s to plot the return of the exiled Stuarts. Wyatt reconstructed the room at a new level as the Stag Parlour but was careful to retain sections from the original overmantel; the new plasterwork was also in a deliberately old-fashioned style and featured a fanciful view of the old house. In the Entrance Hall Wyatt inserted a completely new chimneypiece decorated with plumed helmets and giant broadswords in honour of the Leghs' prowess on the battlefields of the Middle Ages. Prominently displayed in the same room is a full-length portrait of the Black Prince, who had been rescued at the battle of Crécy in 1346 by Sir Thomas Danyers.

36 Questions of Style

(It was to Danyers that the Leghs ultimately owed their ownership of Lyme.) The portrait hangs on hinges so that it can be swung aside to allow a view down from the genuinely Elizabethan Drawing Room into the Entrance Hall.

A similar device features in Sir Walter Scott's Civil War romance *Woodstock* (1826). Through his novels, Scott probably did more than any other early nineteenth-century writer to help to preserve historic interiors and encourage the creation of new ones in a 'Jacobethan' style (see p.162). Almost as important was the artist Joseph Nash, whose *Mansions of England in the Olden Time* (1839–49) provided a pattern-book for the period room. Nash's illustrations, which included the Drawing Room at Lyme Park, brought the past to life with a gusto that masked their numerous anachronisms.

The Elizabethan Inlaid Chamber at Sizergh Castle in Cumbria was also recorded by Nash, who described it as 'the most curious feature of the interior, the panelling of which is inlaid with a profuse expenditure of labour quite peculiar to the decoration of former days'.

By the late nineteenth century many owners of country houses were having to exchange their past for cash. In 1891 the Victoria & Albert Museum bought the panelling from Sizergh's Inlaid Chamber to form its first English period room; it later acquired the gilt toilet service and the four-poster bed from the same room. The negotiations were handled by John Hungerford Pollen, who had advised on the decoration of many historic interiors, including the Long Gallery at Blickling Hall in Norfolk.

Period rooms in museums retain their fascination for many visitors but have fallen from favour with some curators, who see them as inauthentic (although, as we have seen, even in their original setting they can contain a large element of make-believe). The bed, which, like much similar woodwork, is a composite piece of many periods, was loaned back to Sizergh in 1978, and the panelling followed in 1999. The room has been restored to its original setting but has been changed by the experience: artificial lighting has had to be introduced for visitors used to the bright illumination of art galleries.

The fashion for collecting period rooms lasted from the 1890s to the 1920s, and examples can still be seen in the Musée Carnavalet in Paris and the older US museums, such as those in New York, Philadelphia and Boston. Some private owners took a similarly didactic approach. A pioneer was Samuel Rush Meyrick, who in the 1830s decorated a series of rooms at Goodrich Castle in Herefordshire in different period styles to complement his famous collection of armour. Between 1897 and 1914 the Wakefield industrialist Frank Green removed nineteenth-century alterations to the historic interior of Treasurer's House in York to show how he believed the fabric had developed 'from the time of the Romans down to George III'. The rooms in which he displayed his collection of historic English furniture were labelled accordingly: Medieval Great Hall, Tudor Dressing Room, Restoration Room, Vanbrugh Room, William and Mary Staircase, Queen Anne Drawing Room, Georgian Bedroom, Chippendale Bedroom and Sheraton Room. Green stopped living at Treasurer's House in the early 1920s, and, as at Cotehele, the house was turned into a showplace, where the arrangement of the furniture became fossilised. When Green gave the house to the National Trust in 1930, he even nailed studs into the floor to show where every piece should stand.

opposite: **The King's Room – one of the period rooms created by Frank Green at Treasurer's House in York.**

above: **The 'Basildon Room' in the Waldorf Astoria Hotel in New York incorporates Neo-classical decoration salvaged from Basildon Park.**

Country House Style

Britain contains an unrivalled wealth of country houses of different sizes, ages and characters, so it would be absurd to suggest that there could ever be one 'country house style'. Indeed, this book sets out to chart their extraordinary stylistic diversity. Yet the term does still have some meaning and potency. It is not a matter of ornament and decoration but of attitude, linked with notions of what it meant – and sometimes still means – to be a country gentleman. The attitude is summed up in the words 'shabby genteel'. The mellow patina of the old was preferred to the glittery sheen of the new. Clothes and furniture alike were allowed to show honest signs of wear. You must also not appear to try too hard or to flaunt your possessions. So, for instance, at Lyme Park in Cheshire, the 2nd Lord Newton took a perverse delight in denigrating the quality of the Gibbons-style wood-carvings in his Saloon. The perfect expression of this mood is Uppark in West Sussex – or was, until the fire in 1989. It was a house where nothing seemed to have changed since the death of Sir Harry Fetherstonhaugh in 1846. Sun-faded walls and curtains were carefully washed rather than repainted or remade, and gumboots still stood in the Stone Hall. A quiet melancholy prevailed.

When a historic house passed out of private ownership into the care of the National Trust, there was still a general presumption that it should remain a place to live in, not simply a mausoleum for works of art. This point of view was explicitly endorsed by the most successful of all the country-house rescuers, James Lees-Milne, even where he recognised, as when describing Packwood in Warwickshire, that there were some owners who took a very different approach. This house had been created almost from scratch in the 1920s and 1930s by Graham Baron Ash, who had inherited a fortune made in the Birmingham metal industry and retired to a bachelor country life:

If Packwood House looks an immaculate museum today, it was an immaculate museum when Baron lived in it. It never was a proper country house, with worn hats and tobacco pouches in the hall, dogs' baskets and children's toys in the living rooms. Heaven forbid! Baron would have died of horror at the very idea.

Clothes and furniture alike were allowed to show honest signs of wear

left: **The Saloon at Uppark photographed in 1941 in all its faded grandeur.**
opposite: **The Dining Room at Packwood, as furnished by Graham Baron Ash.**

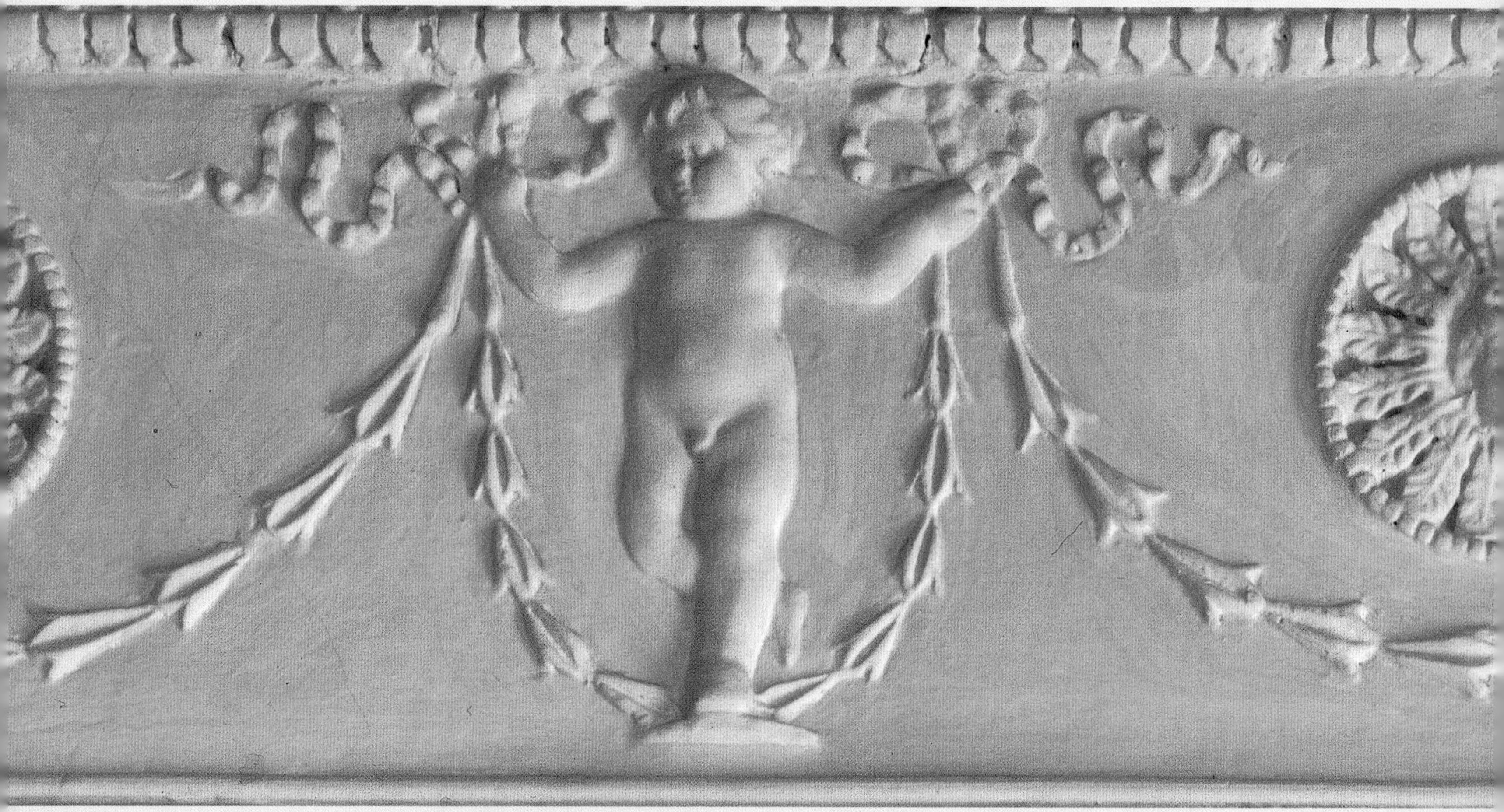

2: Components of Style

42 Components of Style

| Tuscan | Doric | Ionic | Composite | Corinthian |

The Classical Orders

To understand the classical style and its numerous revivals, you first have to understand the classical orders of architecture, which constitute its essential grammar. Indeed, the very word 'style' is thought to be derived from the Greek word for a column, *stylos*.

At their simplest, the orders consist of two elements: a vertical column and a horizontal beam. The column is made up of three parts: plinth, shaft and capital. The beam (or entablature) can also be divided vertically into three parts. Reading from the bottom, they are the architrave, frieze and cornice. The ancient Greeks, who were the first to systematise this combination of column and entablature, recognised three different kinds or orders: Doric, Ionic and Corinthian. The Romans later added two more: Tuscan and Composite. The orders can be most easily distinguished by their capitals, but there are also subtle variations in the proportions of the columns and the components of the entablatures.

The classical orders offered a seemingly simple, but immensely rich and flexible, system of construction, proportion and decoration that could be applied to the articulation of both external façades and internal spaces. The walls of classical interiors are also often subdivided following the principles of the orders: in the Long Gallery at Ham House in Surrey, for example, the cornice is taken from an Ionic entablature, the shaft of the Ionic column establishes the height of the upper wall surface, while the dado is the same height as the plinth.

There were also rules about how the orders should be combined. When superimposed one above another, the example of the Roman Colosseum dictated that Doric had to come at the bottom, Ionic in the middle, and Corinthian at the top. An early, if slightly naïve, example of the orders being superimposed in this way can be seen on the frontispiece of the north front at Lyme Park, which dates from *c*.1570. The pillars supporting the Great Staircase at Knole of *c*.1605 observe exactly the same rules. They still applied when the Colosseum-like frames of the noble gasometers north of King's Cross station were constructed in 1880.

Plain Doric was cheaper to carve and easier to dust than curly Corinthian

As we shall see, architectural theorists have tried to associate individual orders with specific human characteristics or genders – indeed, human figures (known as *caryatids* or *atlantes*) sometimes stand in for the columns – but in practice, the

above: **The Ionic order articulates the panelling in the Long Gallery at Ham House.**
opposite: **The five principal orders, as illustrated in William Chambers's *A Treatise on the Decorative Part of Civil Architecture* (1791).**

choice of which order to use was more often a matter of the designer's taste and the patron's wallet. Plain Doric was cheaper to carve and easier to dust than curly Corinthian.

Since Vitruvius theorists have also tried to provide a definitive canon of the orders, but without success. Imaginative designers have always been more interested in grasping the basic principles (which have never been in doubt) and then breaking the rules for their own purposes. With typical self-confidence, Robert Adam argued that: 'however necessary these rules may be to form the taste and correct the licentiousness of the scholar, they often cramp the genius and circumscribe the ideas of the master.'

Doric

This is first and plainest of the three Greek orders. Greek Doric has a simple, curved moulding for a capital, a squat, fluted column and no base. The Romans invented their own variety of Doric, called Tuscan Doric, which had a slightly more elaborate capital, including egg-and-dart moulding and a concave 'cushion' base (*torus*). Confusingly, they also employed a baseless Doric, which may be distinguished from the Greek original by its slenderer and usually unfluted columns and an extra moulding between the capital and the column shaft. The Temple of Piety at Studley Royal in Yorkshire is a rare example of baseless Roman Doric.

The friezes of all three versions of Doric are divided periodically by three vertical bars (*triglyphs*), which have triangular projections below (*guttae* or 'tears'). Doric seems to derive from earlier wooden construction methods. The *triglyphs* may represent the ends of joists resting on a crossbeam; the *guttae* the wooden pegs that held them in place. Between the *triglyphs* are flat areas known as *metopes*, which are sometimes decorated with *bucrania* (ox-skulls) or *paterae* (rosette-like roundels).

The Doric order was traditionally associated with the warlike Dorians and was seen as essentially masculine in character. As a result, it was often chosen for buildings or rooms associated with male activities. Writing to Lord Kames in 1763, Robert Adam specified Doric as particularly appropriate for entrance halls, which were often decorated in severe stone colours and featured real weapons or plasterwork trophies of arms (see p.68). Adam's Doric was either plain or enriched with decoration in the *metopes*: 'This degree of enrichment I would seldome use without Doors, but is very proper in Halls.' His Neo-classical successors Samuel Wyatt and Henry Holland also adopted Doric for the entrance halls at Shugborough and Berrington Hall.

right: **A screen of Doric columns divides James Wyatt's Entrance Hall at Castle Coole in Co. Fermanagh. Doric was a frequent choice for such severe rooms. Like Adam, Wyatt restricted decoration to the *metopes* of the Doric frieze.**

The Doric order was seen as essentially masculine in character

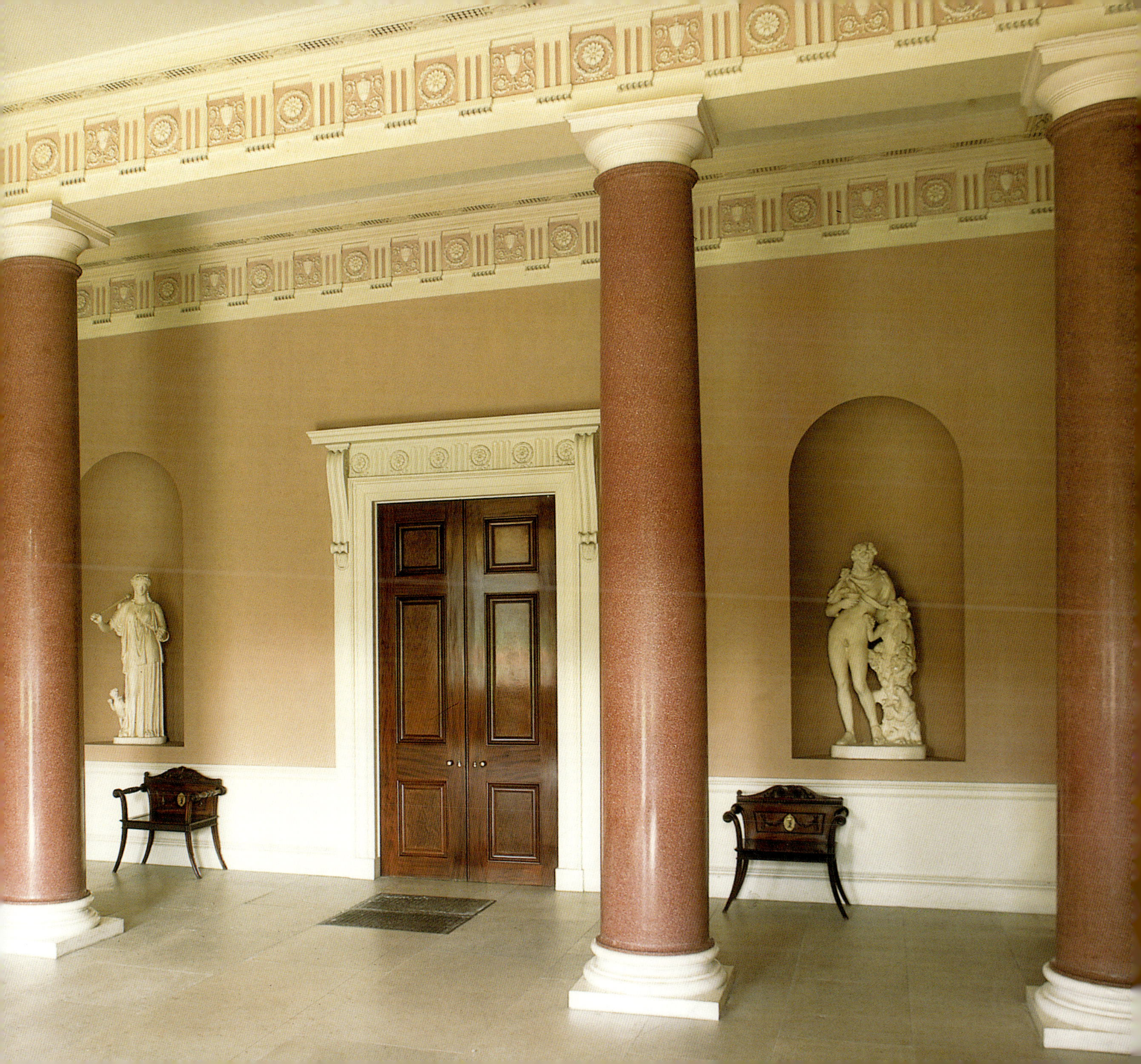

Components of Style

Ionic

The Ionic order is most easily identified by the two ram's-horn-like scrolls on its capital. They are usually separated by a neck (*echinus*) of egg-and-dart moulding. The Ionic frieze is plainer than the Doric, but the architrave and the base are both more complex. The cornice usually includes a row of *dentils* (tooth-like decoration).

The Drawing Room fireplace at Canons Ashby in Northamptonshire incorporates a rare early form of Ionic capital, taken directly from an illustration in Hans Blum's *The Booke of Five Columns*, the first English edition of which was published only in 1601, about the time this fireplace was installed. This was the first book to set out a simple proportional system for the orders, and only the second publication in English on the subject. It was intended 'for the benefit of Freemasons, Carpenters, Goldsmithes, Painters, Carvers, In-layers, Anticke-cutters, and all other [sic] that delight to practice [sic] the Compasse and Squire [set square]'.

The Ionic order was traditionally seen as a feminine complement to the masculine Doric – Vitruvius even compared the two scrolls of its capital to the curly ringlets on a woman's head – so the order was sometimes chosen for boudoirs (such as that at Berrington Hall in Herefordshire), bedrooms and other rooms used by women.

Vitruvius compared the two scrolls of the Ionic capital to the curly ringlets on a woman's head

above: **The Ionic order in the Boudoir at Berrington Hall. It includes swags (p.66) and a Vitruvian scroll (p.71).**
opposite: **The caryatid figures forming the legs of this side-table at Basildon Park, Berkshire, were inspired by the Ionic porch of the Erechtheion on the Athenian Acropolis. The frieze includes curly palmettes (see p.54).**

48 Components of Style

left: **A free-standing Corinthian capital at Anglesey Abbey, Cambridgeshire.**
opposite: **The Saloon chimneypiece at Claydon House represents the Corinthian maiden who is said to have inspired the invention of the order.**

Corinthian

The Corinthian, the most ornate of the Greek orders, is distinguished by its prominent capital, which is made up of curling acanthus leaves that appear to spring from the neck of the column. The Corinthian cornice is slightly more involved than the Ionic, as it includes alternating scrolled brackets and coffering, which are designed to be seen from below.

In ancient Greece the Corinthian order was particularly associated with the interior decoration of buildings that employed the Doric order externally. Corinth was the Dorian city most famous for lavishly decorated interiors at that time. Ever since, designers have chosen the Corinthian order when they wanted to suggest luxury.

The order seems to have originated not in architecture but in metalwork, which could reproduce its complex forms more easily than stone. Vitruvius recorded another more romantic, if less likely, account of its birth. According to this story, the Greek architect Callimachus (c.430–400 BC) was inspired to create the Corinthian capital by seeing an acanthus plant growing through a wicker basket that had been left on the tomb of a Corinthian woman who had died young. The figures supporting the marble chimneypiece in the Saloon at Claydon House in Buckinghamshire were inspired by this tale: on the left, the Corinthian girl holds an example of the capital she inspired; on the right, Callimachus carries a shattered column, symbolising her untimely death.

Tuscan

The unfluted Tuscan column has the squattest proportions of all the orders. It sits on a plain base or has no base at all, and it has a Doric-like capital and an entablature without *triglyphs*.

The order is said to have originated with the Etruscans, who used it for their wooden tomb monuments. It was adopted by the Romans as an even plainer version of the Greek Doric order to proclaim the rustic simplicity of the Roman character in contrast to Greek elegance. As a result, Tuscan was more often chosen for workaday agricultural buildings, such as granaries, or the basement floors of country houses than for luxurious interiors. Lord Chesterfield, writing in 1749, emphasised the point, when he found fault with the crudity of his son's manners:

I dare say you know already enough of architecture, to know that the Tuscan is the strongest of all the orders; but at the same time, it is the coarsest and clumsiest of them. Its solidity does extremely well for the foundation and base-floor of a great edifice; but if the whole building be Tuscan, it will attract no eyes, it will stop no passengers, it will invite no interior examination; people will take it for granted, that the finishing and furnishing cannot be worth seeing, where the front is so unadorned and clumsy. But if upon the solid Tuscan foundation, the Doric, the Ionic, and the Corinthian orders rise gradually with all their beauty, proportions, and ornament, the fabric seizes the most incurious eye. ... Just so will it fare with your little fabric, which at present, I fear, has more of the Tuscan than of the Corinthian order.

'Tuscan is the most solid and the least ornate order ... the most rustic and the most strong' Sebastiano Serlio

Composite

As the name suggests, this style was a composite – of the Ionic and the Corinthian orders. This is seen most clearly in the capital, which combines Ionic scrolls with Corinthian acanthus leaves.

Composite was the only order invented by the Romans, who used it most prominently on the Arch of Titus (built in Rome in the 70s AD), through which the victims of Rome's military conquests were marched in triumph. As a result, the order came to be associated with buildings proclaiming Roman imperial power.

Despite its Roman pedigree, the order was not described by Vitruvius, and the term Composite was not coined until the Renaissance. Thereafter, classical architects used it much less often than the other orders. However, inventive Elizabethan and Jacobean designers were particularly fond of finding exotic variations on it. Good examples can be seen in the Hall at Montacute and the Ballroom at Knole.

opposite: **Tuscan columns flank the Library fireplace at Anglesey Abbey.**

above: **An exotic variation on the Composite capital in the stone screen of the Hall at Montacute.**

right: **Composite pilasters in the Entrance Hall at Beningbrough in Yorkshire.**

Acanthus

The broad, curly and scalloped leaves of the acanthus plant have been one of the most popular forms of ornament since classical times, and the plant itself is still to be seen growing among the classical ruins of the Roman Forum. Arranged vertically side by side, they form an important element in the capitals of the Corinthian and Composite orders (see p.48 and p.51). The leaves are even more widely used when twisted into scrolling patterns. In this form, they give a sense of energy and movement to wall-panels, picture frames, title-page borders and chimney surrounds. They are also often found in heraldic ornament, where they represent the slashed and swirling drapery (known as mantling) that surrounds a coat of arms.

Acanthus scroll ornament was revived during the Italian Renaissance, particularly to decorate tomb chests, and it soon reached northern Europe. It fills many of the Elizabethan carved-wood overmantels at Sizergh Castle in Cumbria and often appears in the engravings of the French designer Jacques Androuet du Cerceau the Elder (c.1510–c.1585), which influenced the rare Elizabethan furniture at Hardwick Hall in Derbyshire.

An especially luxuriant form of open acanthus scroll flourished during the Baroque period, when designers were particularly fond of creating spectacular effects of space and movement. Scrolling acanthus runs up the carved balustrades of many a Baroque staircase – for example, at Dunster Castle in Somerset and Sudbury Hall in Derbyshire (illustrated on p.183). The stately rhythm of the scroll suited the inlaid furniture of the eighteenth-century French designer André-Charles Boulle, and workers in metal found it useful for hiding welding joins.

Neo-classical designers, such as Robert Adam, favoured a slimmer type of acanthus scroll, which covers the walls of Adam's Eating Room at Osterley Park in Middlesex. The scrolls were sometimes arranged in pairs and so severely pruned that their origins in the acanthus leaf are not immediately apparent. This type, sometimes known as *rinceaux* (French for foliate scrolls), appears in the French Neo-classical wall decoration of the Boudoir at Attingham Park in Shropshire (illustrated on p.129).

Scrolling acanthus runs up the carved balustrades of many a Baroque staircase

Perhaps not surprisingly for an advocate of all things Gothic, the early Victorian architect A.W.N. Pugin deplored the ubiquity of this classical ornament in his book *The True Principles* (1841). It was left to William Morris to revive the acanthus by returning to its vegetable origins with his 'Acanthus' pattern wallpaper of 1875 (illustrated on p.164).

above: **This engraved acanthus frieze was designed by Edward Pierce. Published in 1640, it was the first ornament design by an English artist to rival the best of continental work. Pierce's son used this pattern when carving the staircase balustrade at Sudbury Hall in 1676 (illustrated on p.183).**

Anthemion

This stylised floral ornament may have been based on the flower of the honeysuckle. (The word comes from the Greek for flower, *anthos*.) The anthemion was used both vertically, as a central element on panels of grotesque or acanthus ornament (illustrated opposite), and horizontally, in bands, alternating with stylised lotus leaves or palmettes (palm leaves, see below). The anthemion and palmette are similar and are sometimes used as interchangeable terms, but, according to some authorities, they may be distinguished by the open petals of the former.

The anthemion is a ubiquitous component of classical decoration. It appears on the neck of the capital of the Ionic order and also on numerous Greek vases. Neo-classical designers, such as James 'Athenian' Stuart and Robert Adam, made much use of it in all forms of decoration, from plasterwork ceilings and wall-panels, wrought-iron railings and open chairbacks, to stencilled friezes and floors.

This simple motif offered considerable variety in the ways it could be used. In the late eighteenth century anthemion petals were sometimes almost as serrated as acanthus leaves. In Art Deco ornament they are stripped down to the simplest outline.

This simple motif offered considerable variety in the ways it could be used

left: Anthemions between lotus leaves in the marquetry border of a table-top at Belton House in Lincolnshire.
right: The open-leaved anthemion alternates with the closed-leaved palmette (below) in the window reveals of the Saloon at Uppark, West Sussex.

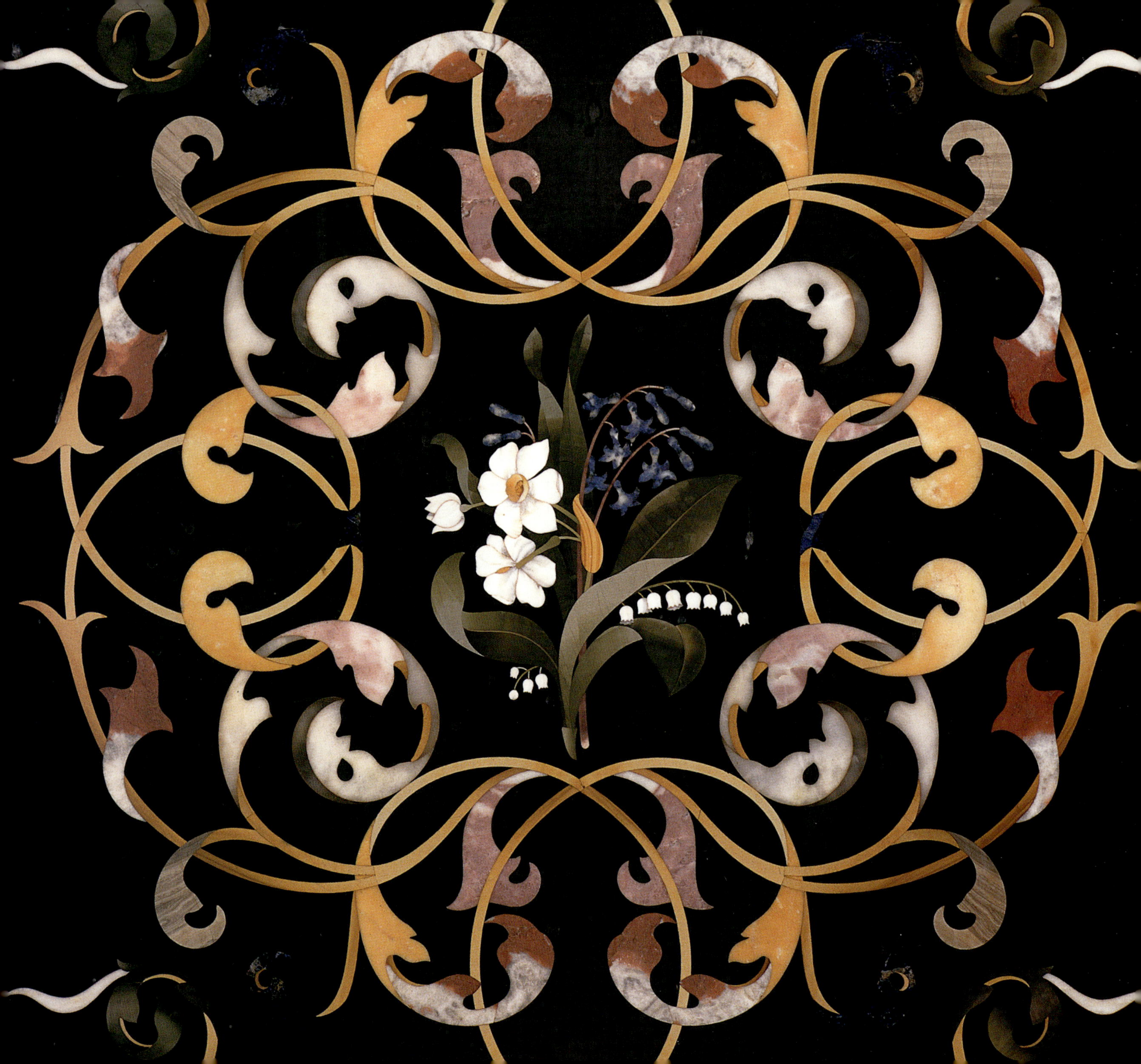

Arabesque

A stylised pattern of curling and interlaced foliage, an arabesque somewhat resembles the intertwining tendrils of a clematis. Although it does not spring from a single stem, it is usually symmetrical about a central point and in theory can be infinitely extended outwards. Unlike grotesque ornament (see p.60), it does not usually include figurative elements.

As the name suggests, the arabesque originated in the Arab Near East, where it was particularly used as an engraved decoration on metalwork. In the early sixteenth century the motif was taken up by Venetian publishers, who often combined it with strapwork (see p.64) on title-page cartouches and bindings. Ornament prints also helped to spread the taste for the arabesque throughout Europe.

Arabesque decoration proved immensely popular for the next 200 years, as it was so easy to adapt to different media and mix with other decorative motifs. The fine curling lines of the arabesque were especially suitable for inlay, whether it was in jewellery, metalwork or furniture. On the larger scale, it proved ideal to ornament wrought-iron gates and screens from the late seventeenth century onwards. The 'seaweed' marquetry that decorates many fine late seventeenth-century cabinets is a frilly variation on the arabesque pattern.

The Renaissance Revival of the mid-nineteenth century (see p.160) revived interest in the arabesque. Particularly good examples animate the *pietra dura* panelling in the Spanish Room at Kingston Lacy.

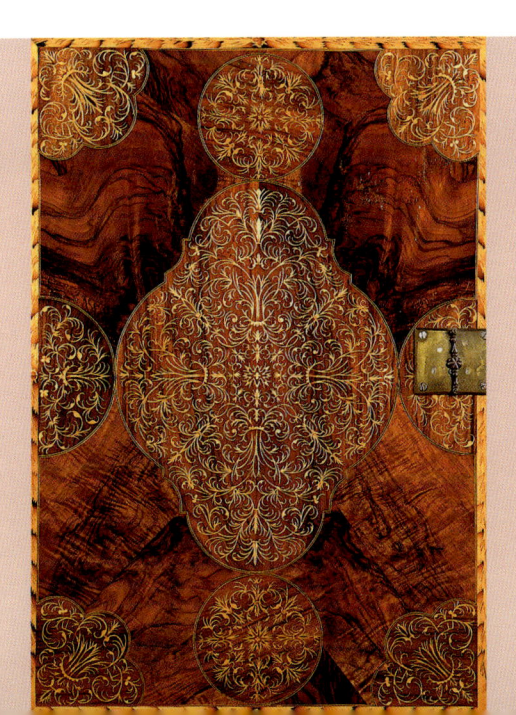

The fine curling lines of the arabesque were especially suitable for inlay

left: **This 'seaweed' marquetry panel of c.1690 at Canons Ashby, Northamptonshire, employs the frilliest form of the arabesque pattern.**

above: **The Earl of Surrey's doublet is embroidered with arabesque patterns in this posthumous portrait of c.1550 at Knole in Kent.**

opposite: **Arabesque tendrils encircle a sprig of flowers on one of the *pietra dura* cabinets in the Spanish Room at Kingston Lacy in Dorset.**

Cartouche

A panel, tablet or shield (usually bearing an inscription or coat of arms) and the frame that encloses it is known as a cartouche. It is normally rectangular or oval in form.

Sixteenth- and early seventeenth-century cartouches made much use of curling strapwork (see p.65). They reached the height of swelling sophistication in the Baroque period, when they often appear framing coats of arms within broken pediments, both above fireplaces and over doorways, as at Canons Ashby in Northamptonshire. Other examples can be seen over the bed in the State Bedroom at Powis Castle, proclaiming the family's loyalty to the Stuarts, and in stone in the Queen's Room at Sudbury Hall in Derbyshire. The latter is by Sir William Wilson in the style of Grinling Gibbons, who was a master at carved-wood cartouches, often combined with swags (see p.66).

The asymmetrical, shell-like cartouche is one of the defining characteristics of the early eighteenth-century Rococo style (see p.106), which applied it particularly to ornament engravings. Rex Whistler made great play with the motif in his Rococo Revival murals of the 1930s.

Neo-classical designers returned to extremely plain cartouches as frames for classical inscriptions. They were usually rectangular and tablet-like in form with wedge-shaped terminations to left and right.

> They often appear framing coats of arms within broken pediments

above: **A florid cartouche frames the monogram of Charles I or II in the State Bedroom at Powis Castle.**

Griffin

The mythical beast has the head, wings and talons of an eagle and the body of a lion. It is usually shown seated and in profile and often with its mirror-image pair.

In legend, the creature is associated with light and fire, and so it made an appropriate appearance in the vertical bands of 'candelabra' ornament developed by Neo-classical designers out of Raphael's grotesques (see p.61). Adam often also used pairs of griffins on chairs and as cresting for his mirrors, but it is doubtful whether they had any symbolic significance for him. However, the griffin ornament in the Entrance Hall at Basildon Park in Berkshire may have meant something particular to its creator, Sir Francis Sykes, as he had made his money in India, and griffins were traditionally said to have guarded all the gold of the Subcontinent.

right: **A pair of griffins on a mosaic table at Charlecote Park.**

The creature is associated with light and fire

60 Components of Style

'The bones of a Rammes head hung with strings of beads and Ribands, Satyres, Tritons, apes, Cornucopia'

Henry Peacham, 1606

Grotesque

This type of ornament takes its name from the Roman wall-paintings discovered in 1488 during the excavation of the *Domus Aurea*, the Emperor Nero's 'Golden House' in Rome. Such buried chambers were known as grottoes, and their decoration as *grottesci*, or 'grotesques'.

Grotesque ornament usually incorporates curling scrolls and swags, tablets and roundels, shrines and candelabra, human figures, and real and mythical beasts, such as griffins – all piled one above another in vertically symmetrical panels. The playful and fantastic quality of this decoration – so different from the sobriety of the classical orders – appealed to Renaissance artists such as Raphael, who in 1518–20 decorated the pilasters of the Vatican *Loggie* (covered arcades) with grotesque decoration that proved immensely influential. It was transmitted via ceramics and engravings to northern Europe, where, combined with strapwork, it achieved its most grotesque form (in the modern sense), becoming an important component of the Jacobean style (see p.80).

In late seventeenth-century France the designer Jean Bérain (see p.94) developed a lighter version of the grotesque, and this was very influential on Rococo artists, who adapted the motifs, while abandoning the essential symmetry of their arrangement. Neo-classical and Renaissance Revival designers returned for inspiration to the original Roman murals, many more of which were uncovered at Pompeii and Herculaneum in the mid-eighteenth century. J.D. Crace's Pompeian Room at Ickworth (see p.132) makes plentiful use of grotesques.

opposite: **A mid-sixteenth-century Limoges enamel charger at Powis Castle.**

right: **The vertical panels of carved grotesque ornament in the Cartoon Gallery at Knole were painted by Paul Isaacson** *c.*1608.

Guilloche

The word guilloche (pronounced 'ghee-osh') derives from the French word, which means 'chequer pattern', but the decoration referred to by this name consists of a continuous band of twisted strands – something slightly different.

The motif seems to be Assyrian in origin, but it became ubiquitous in Greek and Roman decoration, particularly in mosaics. The mosaic borders at Chedworth Roman Villa in Gloucestershire, which were probably laid in the late third or early fourth century AD, contain the simplest form of guilloche, consisting of two twisted strands, and also the three-strand plait form. The guilloche motif was revived at the Renaissance and appears in every subsequent classical revival, but in its simplest plaited form it is evident anywhere that strands of material are twisted together – in rope, knitted textiles, jewellery, plaited hair and even bread.

It was much used in the mouldings of Restoration plasterwork ceilings (see p.86) and Renaissance Revival houses such as Kingston Lacy in Dorset, where it borders the carved-wood doors in the Dining Room. Guilloche in the form of gilded rope is even incorporated into the frieze of the Golden Room.

Neo-classical designers often developed the motif by inserting roses or simple circles at the centre of each 'loop'.

It is evident anywhere that strands of material are twisted together

above and opposite: **Variations on the guilloche motif form the borders of the mosaic floors at Chedworth Roman Villa.**

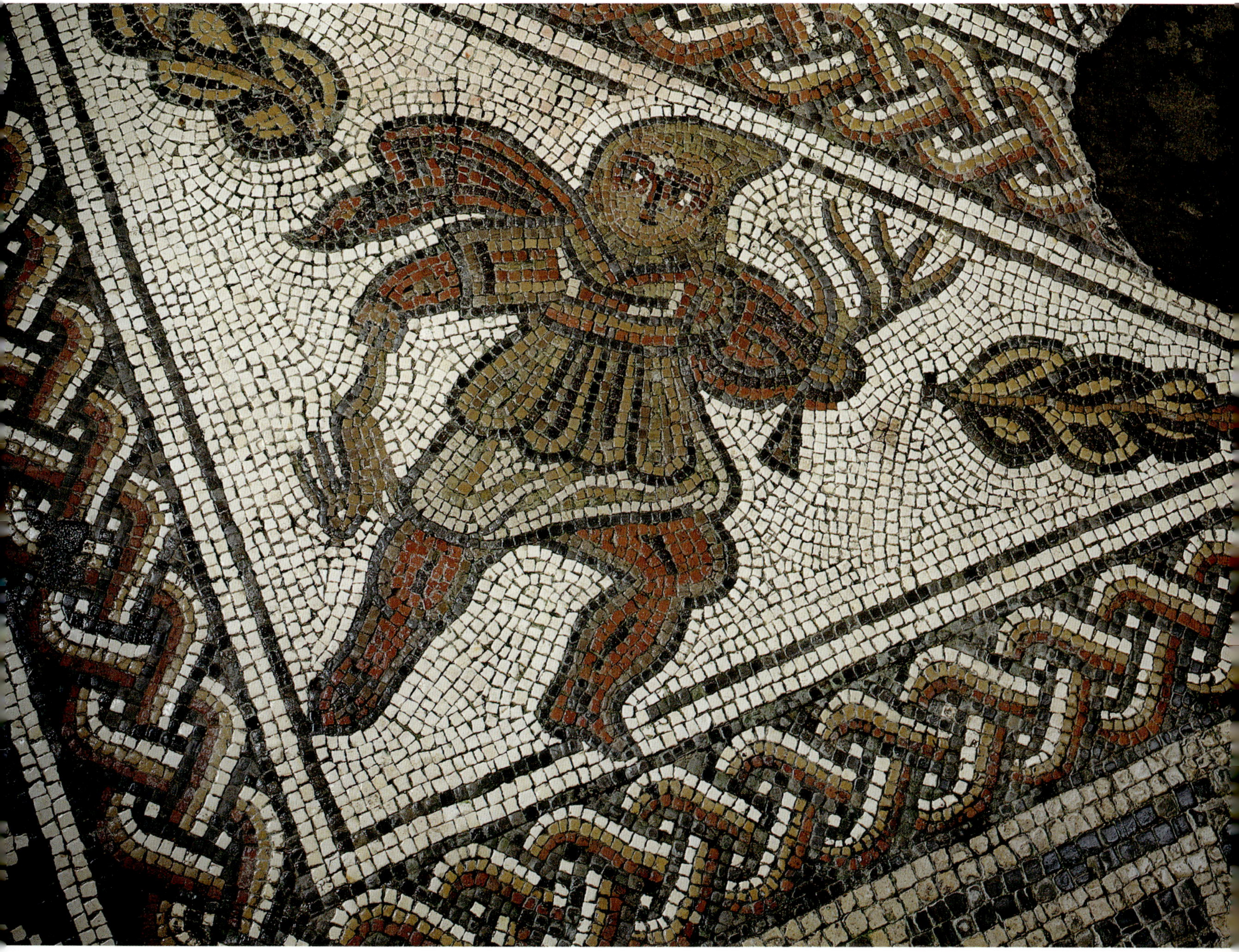

64 Components of Style

Strapwork

The ornament consists of a pattern of bands, or straps, which appear to have been cut out from a thick but flexible material, such as leather, and then twisted or curled. Intersections in the pattern are usually marked by punched holes and protrusions somewhat resembling the semicircular gable ends of a Jacobean building. Strapwork often provides a framework through which more fluid arabesque decoration can be woven.

Strapwork is said to have been invented by the Italian Mannerist painter Rosso Fiorentino (1494–1540), who first used it in the plaster frieze of the Gallery of François I at the château of Fontainebleau in 1533–5. It was especially popular in northern Europe in the late sixteenth and early seventeenth centuries and was a key element in the Jacobean style (see p.80). It was much used in low-relief plasterwork, both on ceilings, like that of the Long Gallery at Blickling Hall in Norfolk, and for overmantel cartouches, like that in the King Charles Room at Dunster Castle in Somerset. But it could also be applied to furniture (most notably, *sgabello* chairs; see p.82), to textiles (the hangings of the spangle bed at Knole) and to openwork (the cresting over the Great Hall screen at Montacute in Somerset).

Strapwork was revived in the nineteenth century as part of the Renaissance Revival and Jacobethan styles, so it features prominently in the Drawing Room chimneypiece at Cragside and on the chair-covers in the Library at Charlecote.

opposite: **This Elizabethan cushion cover at Hardwick Hall is decorated with strapwork cut out of cloth of silver.**

below: **Strapwork decoration frames a screaming head on the Great Hall screen at Knole.**

Swag

A swag (or festoon) is the curving form created by suspending a cord loosely between two fixed and level points. The cord is usually decorated with flowers and fruit, and the motif may originally have been inspired by temporary floral decorations of the kind seen in Roman murals and still put up for Christmas at Cotehele and Lanhydrock in Cornwall.

Such curving forms were a useful antidote to the essentially rectilinear framework of the classical orders, and they were much used in the *metopes* of the Doric frieze. They also feaure in an Ionic frieze at Berrington (see p.47). The motif arrived in Britain with the Renaissance. A particularly good early example appears on the sarcophagus tomb of Sir Robert Dormer (d.1552) of Ascott in Buckinghamshire. It reached the height of sophistication with the limewood carvings of Grinling Gibbons, who transformed swags of fruit, flowers, dead birds and fish into miracles of fluid rhythm and undercutting.

The form was revived in much simpler form by Adam and other Neo-classical designers, who often used thin strings of husks (rather than fruit and flowers), held up by standing putti (see p.40). They applied it both decoratively and with a practical purpose – for instance, for the metal drop-handles on drawer fronts.

The curving shape of the swag determines the way loose draperies are arranged in many historic interiors, most obviously on the testers of state beds and the pelmets of window curtains. 'Festooning' can also be a sign of neglect: when hanging textiles start to unravel, gravity dictates that they naturally adopt this shape.

left: Carved swags of fruit and foliage in the style of Grinling Gibbons at Belton House.

opposite: Swag carved by Edward Pierce the Younger for the Saloon at Sudbury Hall.

'An Ornament of Flowers, employed in Borders and Decorations'
William Aglionby, 1685

Trophy

Originally a symbolic representation of military victory, consisting of an assemblage of weapons – shields, swords, helmets and breastplates – often in low relief, the trophy was later used to represent other themes, such as hunting, the seasons and the peaceful arts.

Victorious Greek warriors hung the captured weapons of their enemies in trees, and the Romans made similar memorials in stone. In medieval Britain weapons were often hung on the walls of entrance halls so that they would be ready to hand in time of trouble. There was, therefore, both classical and native sanction for incorporating the motif of the military trophy into the decoration of one's home.

When the eighteenth-century owner of medieval Cotehele in Cornwall wished to emphasise its ancient character, real weapons that had long fallen out of use were arranged decoratively in the entrance hall. In 1708–10 in the hall at Canons Ashby Edward Dryden installed a large panel painted with representations of contemporary weapons but with a similar antiquarianising motive. Neo-classical designers, such as Robert Adam and Henry Holland, recalled this tradition but naturally reverted to classical models when they put plasterwork trophies of arms on the walls of the entrance halls at Castle Ward, Osterley Park and Berrington Hall. Such trophies were not restricted to entrance halls: they appear, for instance, on the pilasters painted *c.*1608 by Paul Isaacson in the Cartoon Gallery at Knole.

From the seventeenth century the trophy format was extended not only to related activities, such as hunting, but also to completely different themes that had become popular with designers and that lent themselves to symbolic representation in this form: love, the arts, the seasons, pastoral life and so on. Typical are the limewood trophies on these themes in the style of Grinling Gibbons at Lyme Park.

The modern sports trophy recalls the three-dimensional form and competitive significance of the original classical trophy.

Weapons were often hung on the walls of entrance halls so they would be ready to hand in time of trouble

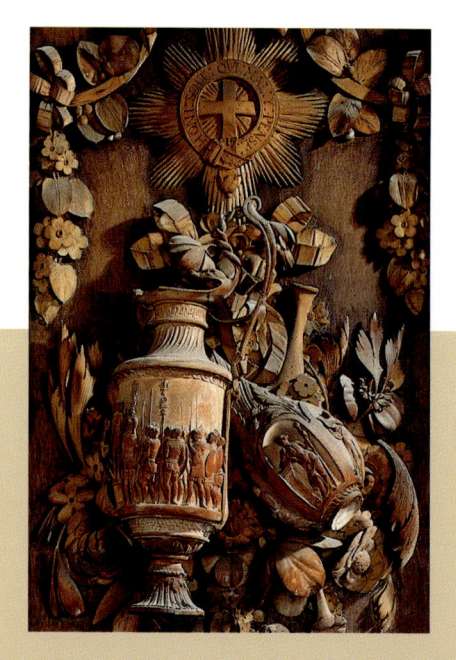

above: **Gibbons's superb limewood carvings at Petworth include trophies of classical urns.**
opposite: **A Neo-classical trophy designed by Henry Holland for the Entrance Hall of Berrington Hall.**

69

70 Components of Style

Vitruvian scrolls often feature in staircase halls

Vitruvian Scroll

This scrolling pattern resembles a row of rolling waves in profile and so is sometimes known as a 'wave scroll' or, more obscurely, as a 'running dog scroll'. Its connection with the Roman architect and codifier of the classical orders, Vitruvius, is not clear. The 'waves' usually run horizontally, from left to right, but sometimes form mirrored halves meeting in the centre of the piece.

Vitruvian scrolls appear in the mosaics at Chedworth Roman Villa and wherever classical ornament is used. Roman designers developed the motif by adding foliage to form the acanthus scroll (see p.52). Vitruvian scrolls often feature in staircase halls to divide floors, as at Belton House in Lincolnshire and at Peckover House in Cambridgeshire. They were especially popular with late eighteenth-century Neo-classical designers, who applied them to friezes and borders.

opposite: **Vitruvian scrolls run up the side of the main stairs and across the wall at first-floor level at Belton House.**

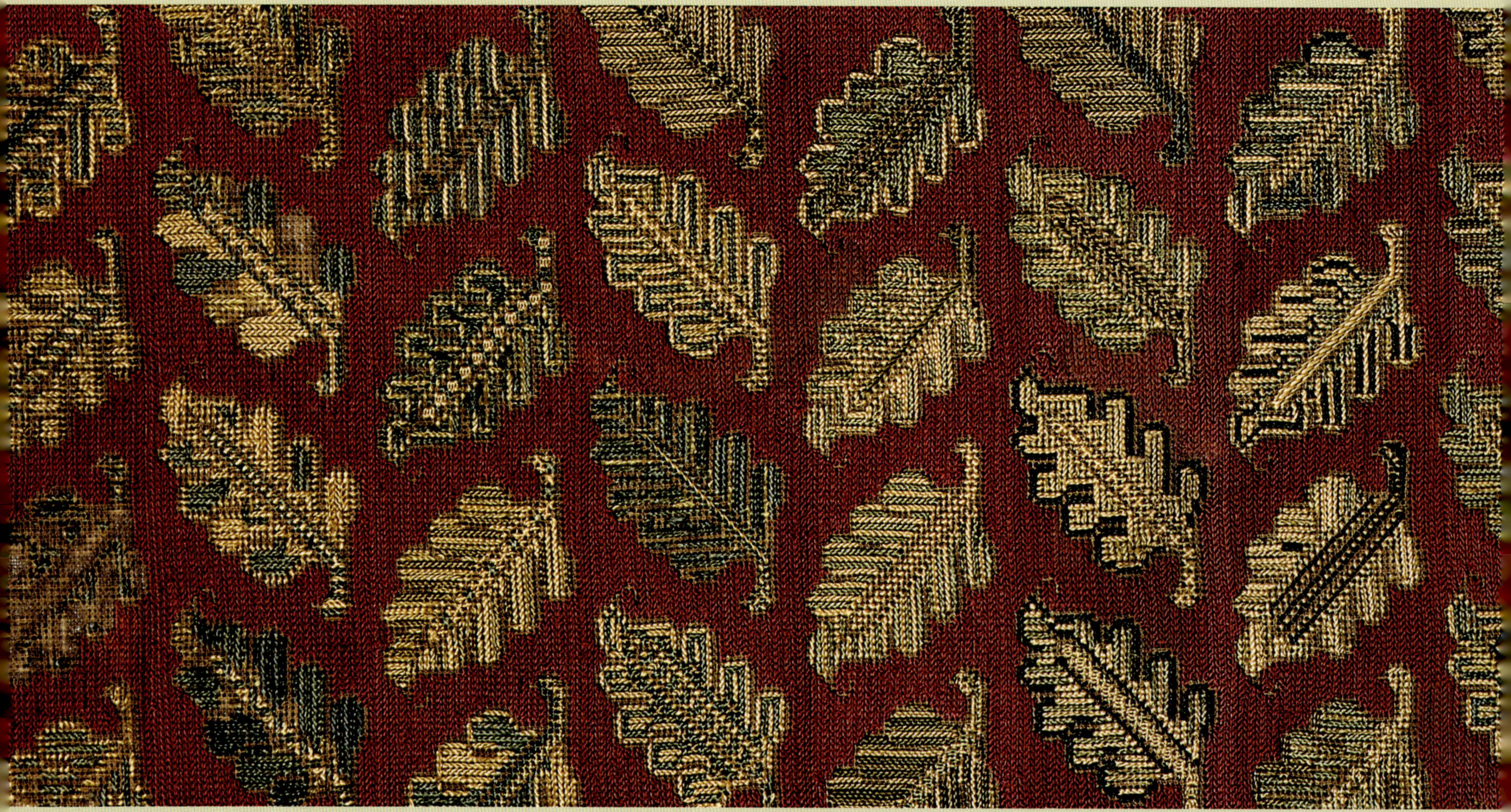

3: Historical Styles and Designers

'Terms of art, which are as inescapable as they are unsatisfactory'

Roy Porter, *Enlightenment*, 2000

Renaissance

Renaissance simply means 'rebirth' or 'revival'. In the history of style, this has happened many times in many eras, but the term is most commonly applied to the rediscovery of classical antiquity in fifteenth-century Italy and the spread of these ideas slightly later to northern Europe.

Renaissance style was absorbed into English culture only slowly and hesitantly, through ornament engravings or immigrant artists. At the height of his power in the early 1520s Cardinal Wolsey brought over the Florentine Renaissance sculptor Giovanni da Maiano to work on his new mansion at Hampton Court. Maiano produced a series of roundels containing busts of classical worthies in floral frames with classical egg-and-dart inner mouldings, one of which has found its way to The Vyne. But few other Italian Renaissance artists made the long journey to England.

Maiano cast his roundels in terracotta, a material that proved particularly suited to reproducing complex grotesque ornament, one of the most characteristic rediscoveries of the Italian Renaissance (see p.60). When Margaret Bedingfeld of Oxburgh Hall died in 1514, she left money for a memorial in the village church. The Ionic pilasters and the panels between them are smothered in a riot of grotesque decoration, all cast in terracotta. This type of ornament, which was then known as 'anticke worke', was described by Henry Peacham in his *Graphice* (1606): 'The forme of it is a generall and … an unnaturall or unorderly composition for delight sake, of men, beasts, birds, fishes, flowers.' It is unclear exactly when the Bedingfeld monument was set up in this remote Norfolk church or who commissioned it. Margaret's son was a member of Henry VIII's court, but could it have been her grandson, Sir Henry Bedingfeld, who was a protégé of the Duke of Northumberland? For a brief period in the 1550s the Protestant circle of Northumberland and his rival, Protector Somerset, built houses that showed a new, more sophisticated understanding of French Renaissance classicism. This circle included Sir Robert Dormer, an early owner of Ascott, whose tomb in Wing church uses the classical language with immense assurance: fluted Corinthian columns, egg-and-dart mouldings, *bucrania* (ox-skulls) and swags. Another member was Sir William Sharington, who added the octagonal tower to Lacock Abbey in Wiltshire around 1550. Still inside it is the stone table he commissioned, which is carved with acanthus leaf scrolls and other classical mouldings.

'An unnaturall or unorderly composition for delight sake, of men, beasts, birds, fishes, flowers'

above: **Margaret Bedingfeld's terracotta monument in Oxborough church is covered with Renaissance grotesque ornament.**
left: **Giovanni da Maiano's terracotta roundel at The Vyne was one of the first Italian Renaissance sculptures to reach Britain.**
right: **Sir William Sharington's stone table at Lacock Abbey.**

For the Tudor courtier Renaissance culture was as much a matter of words as images. Henry Howard, Earl of Surrey, introduced Italian Renaissance poetry in the form of the Petrarchan sonnet to England. Shortly after he was executed in 1547, a portrait was commissioned that shows him as a true Renaissance man. (A later copy now hangs at Knole, part of which is illustrated on p.57.) His doublet is embroidered with arabesque ornament in the Italian style, and he leans his arm on a broken classical column, symbolising life cut short.

76 Historical Styles and Designers

The Tudor rose was the ubiquitous symbol of authority and badge of loyalty

above: **Sir Thomas More and his Family,** by Rowland Lockey after Hans Holbein (Nostell Priory).

right: **The Tudor painted ceiling at Ightham Mote displays the Tudor rose, Beaufort portcullis and castle of Castile (for Henry VIII's Spanish first wife).**

opposite: **The Tudor linenfold panelling in the Oak Gallery at The Vyne incorporates a huge range of heraldic and other emblems.**

Tudor

During the Tudor era (1485–1603) there was a gradual stylistic evolution from the last phase of medieval Gothic (represented supremely by the Perpendicular of King's College Chapel, Cambridge, which Henry VIII completed) towards the northern version of the Renaissance in its most ornamental form (sometimes known as Mannerism).

One of the key figures in introducing the northern Renaissance style to the English court was the German painter Hans Holbein (?1497–1543). His portrait *Sir Thomas More and his Family* probably does not represent an actual interior and is now known only through later copies, but it gives us some sense of what the home of a leading early Tudor courtier would have looked like in the late 1520s. More himself wears the emblems of the Tudors. His chain is formed from the Lancastrian double SS motif (he was at the time Chancellor of the Duchy of Lancaster). The clasp is the portcullis symbol of Henry VIII's grandmother, Lady Margaret Beaufort, which was later adopted as the motif of Parliament, and from it hangs the Tudor rose, which became the ubiquitous symbol of authority and badge of loyalty. Both portcullis and rose also appear on the painted ceiling of the Tudor chapel at Ightham Mote in Kent.

Canopies also symbolised authority, and in Holbein's painting one is placed over a two-tier buffet or sideboard, which was an equally prestigious piece of Tudor furniture. For the Tudors oriental carpets were too valuable to be used just as floor coverings, and so they were often thrown over tables, as here. The elaborate flower arrangements are depicted with botanical accuracy and were probably taken from life rather than prints, as the version of Holbein's picture at Nostell Priory shows peonies and other introductions of that period. Hanging from the coffered ceiling above More is a weight-driven lantern clock of the kind that first brought the accurate telling of time into the sixteenth-century home. A similar wall clock is depicted in the late sixteenth-century mural of an interior at Canons Ashby in Northamptonshire.

In the right-hand corner is an internal porch. In an era before corridors were common, when rooms often opened directly into one another, this was a useful device to provide privacy and reduce draughts. Slightly later examples can still be seen at Montacute in Somerset and Sizergh Castle in Cumbria. They have also been re-created at Lytes Cary in Somerset and Lodge Park in Gloucestershire. The cresting along the top is formed from fleur-de-lis (from the royal coat of arms, where they symbolise the weakening Tudor claim to France) and shield-bearing beasts, which also appear in more ferocious form on the Jacobean staircase at Knole.

At Sizergh and elsewhere such porches are often articulated with the classical orders. Here, a more old-fashioned form of decoration is used: linenfold panelling. Representing stiffly folded pieces of linen, usually set vertically, these carved-wood panels are said to have originated in fifteenth-century Flanders. They were applied to furniture and, most commonly, to the walls of small but important rooms. Tapestries were generally preferred for the walls of larger rooms. Such panelling was often moved around, but perhaps the most complete and unaltered example of an early Tudor linenfold panelled room is the Oak Gallery at The Vyne in Hampshire, where it is combined with a huge assortment of heraldic and other devices. This long gallery was itself a Tudor innovation – a room in which to hang family portraits, walk on wet days and look out down on a formal garden. (What is said to be More's Chelsea garden appears in another version of the Holbein family portrait.)

Elizabethan

above: **Mary, Queen of Scots worked this needlework panel at Oxburgh Hall with a symbolic representation of a favourite Latin motto.**
below: **The 'sea-dog' table at Hardwick Hall.**

Although Elizabeth I herself built little, she encouraged her subjects to do so, and through numerous portraits she stamped her face on the age. In the Long Gallery at Hardwick Hall in Derbyshire hangs a rare full-length image of the queen, which was created – like the house – in the 1590s. She wears a dress encrusted with pearls and embroidered with flowers and animals, which seem at first sight simply to be decoration but each of which carries its own message.

The Elizabethans were fascinated by 'devices' or 'conceits' – distilled words or images that concealed some hidden, often complex meaning – and incorporated them into every aspect of their lives. Here, the spring flowers evoke the eternal spring of the Golden Age, with which Elizabeth's reign was compared. Poets likened the queen to Astraea, the virgin goddess of that Golden Age, whose return promised everlasting spring. The single white eglantine rose – also the crest of the Hardwick family – symbolises the chastity of the Virgin Queen. The embroidered animals range from the familiar white swan (symbolising female beauty) to fabulous horned sea-monsters.

Actual Elizabethan embroideries showing a similar love of symbolism survive at Hardwick and at Oxburgh Hall in Norfolk, some made by the creator of Hardwick, Bess, Countess of Shrewsbury, and her royal prisoner, Mary, Queen of Scots. Mary lamented her fate with the needle: one panel depicts a knife pruning a vine with her favourite motto: VIRESCIT VULNERE VIRTUS ('Virtue flourishes with a wound'). In another, Bess mourned the death of her second husband, Sir William Cavendish, by including falling tears and snapped mourning rings, together with the Cavendish stag and serpent.

Devices were used to decorate buildings right across the religious spectrum. The Catholic Sir Thomas Tresham incorporated the symbols of Christ's passion into the frieze of his unfinished house at Lyveden New Bield in Northamptonshire, which itself took the form of a Christian cross. Some 35 miles away, at Canons Ashby, the Puritan Sir Erasmus Dryden covered the walls of the Winter Parlour with the emblems of friends and neighbours, set within simple strapwork frames and borders resembling decidedly un-Puritan jewellery.

Fantastic beasts like those on Elizabeth's skirt also feature in perhaps the most famous of the few surviving pieces of Elizabethan furniture – the 'sea-dog' table at Hardwick. The heads are canine, possibly referring to the 'talbot' hounds that supported the coat of arms of Bess's fourth husband, George Talbot, 6th Earl of Shrewsbury. However, the rest of the bodies are chimeras, mythical winged sea-creatures that can swim, fly and walk. Swags similar to those on the tomb of Sir Robert Dormer (see p.74) hang round their necks and on the sides of the table. The speedy chimeras rest on more slow-moving tortoises, perhaps illustrating the motto *Festina lente* ('hasten slowly'). The creatures seem to be based on an engraving by the French designer, Jacques Androuet du Cerceau the Elder, but it is not clear whether they were made in England or France.

right: **Queen Elizabeth I's skirt is richly embroidered with emblematic beasts and flowers in this portrait at Hardwick.**

The flowers evoke the eternal spring of the Golden Age, with which Elizabeth's reign was compared

Jacobean

This style takes its name from the Latin form of James I's name, *Jacobus*. The greatest decorative creations produced during his reign (1603–25) were purely temporary – the complex stage sets for the court masques and state ceremonials – and the man responsible for making many of these was William Portington, Master Carpenter of the King's Works between 1579 and 1629. For Ben Jonson's *Masque of Beauty*, which was first performed for the court in 1608, he managed to construct a 'floating island', which moved across the stage, carrying a 'throne of beauty' and a host of cupids, which revolved in the opposite direction. In 1612 he also designed the 'great stately hearse' for the funeral of Henry, Prince of Wales, which consisted of a pyramid covered with royal symbols and supported on six Doric columns; within it was a lifelike effigy of the dead prince, complete with moving limbs.

All this has long since disappeared, but Portington's equally remarkable work for Thomas Sackville, 1st Earl of Dorset at Knole has survived. In 1603–8 he created the elaborate oak panelling for the Great Chamber (now the Ballroom), where the earl would have entertained important guests with food, music and dancing. The panelling is articulated by Composite pilasters, the shafts of which are decorated with strapwork, derived – like so much Elizabethan and Jacobean ornament – from Flemish engravings, in this case an illustration in Hans Vredeman de Vries's *Architectura* (1565); from the capitals spring winged horses and scowling masks, like the screaming faces that run round the room at a lower level. Above is the even richer frieze, carved with pairs of mermaids holding celebratory wreaths

> Here the magical world of Shakespeare's *A Midsummer Night's Dream* is given decorative form

left: **Mermaids and hippocamps (a form of sea-horse) feature in William Portington's carved frieze in the Ballroom at Knole.**
right: **A carved pilaster reused from the original Jacobean staircase at Blickling Hall.**

over Tudor roses (Sackville was a cousin of the late queen), hippocamps (mythical relations of the sea-dogs in the Hardwick table) and squatting figures, their cloven feet clamped to the wall with manacles that borrow from the language of strapwork. Here the magical world of Shakespeare's *A Midsummer Night's Dream* (first performed about 1595–6) is given decorative form.

Another royal craftsman, Cornelius Cure, was responsible for the vast chimneypiece and overmantel in the same room, which is one of the masterpieces of Jacobean classicism. Between the Ionic columns the lintel of local grey marble is carved with luxuriant acanthus scrolls. In the overmantel black marble provides the background for the exquisite alabaster garlands of flowers, ribbons and musical instruments, which frame the central strapwork cartouche. The pattern of the panelling is echoed in the ribs of Richard Dungan's plasterwork ceiling, within which are set foliage and single flowers, probably derived from printed herbals. Dungan's designs for Knole subsequently appeared in Walter Gedde's *Booke of Sundry Draughtes* (1616).

Caroline

This term is now little used to describe the art of the reign of Charles I (1625–49), which is a pity, because the king was a passionate patron and collector, who had a profound influence on the visual culture of his era. He also probably knew more about art than any other British monarch.

The image that Charles and his court wished to project is preserved most memorably in the portraiture of Sir Anthony Van Dyck (1599–1641). A sophisticated, nonchalant and (with hindsight) melancholy figure looks out from Van Dyck's portrait of the king hanging in the Long Gallery at Ham House in Surrey. Unusually, this picture still has its original carved frame, which is in the auricular style – that is, the curving, S-scroll decoration appears to have been pressed flat and squeezed into forms that vaguely resemble the human ear. Many of the other contemporary portraits in the Long Gallery have auricular frames, also known as 'Sunderland' frames, after the 2nd Earl of Sunderland (1640–1702), who particularly favoured them, although the style seems to have originated in Holland: Anglo-Dutch frames of about 1640 in this style hang on the staircase at Ham. The auricular style was most fully developed by Adriaen van Vianen and other Dutch goldsmiths working in Haarlem around 1600, and its fluid forms were taken up again 150 years later by Rococo designers (see p.106).

The Ham Long Gallery was remodelled in 1639 for Charles I's boyhood friend, William Murray, and the style of its panelling shows how much advanced taste had moved on since the Knole Ballroom decoration of 1603–8 (see p.81). The decisive factor was the architect Inigo Jones (1573–1652), who had visited Italy in 1613–14 and introduced to Britain a much deeper understanding of classical Roman architecture, based on the buildings, drawings and writings of Andrea Palladio (see p.100). Gone are the strapwork, screaming faces and mythical beasts; instead, panelling is arranged in plain rectangular fields and divided by fluted Ionic pilasters, which support a simple but complete classical entablature of architrave, frieze and cornice. The only enrichment to the joinery is partial gilding.

left: **The *sgabello* chairs at Lacock Abbey were probably designed by Franz Clein.**

The adjoining Green Closet is an even rarer surviving example of Caroline decoration. William Murray refurbished this intimate cabinet in 1637–9 to display his collection of miniatures, which – yet more remarkably – is also still here. The ceiling decoration was inspired by easel paintings from Charles I's own collection in the style of the High Renaissance master, Raphael. The painter of this ceiling was Franz Clein, or Francis Cleyn when anglicised (1582–1658), who also ran the Mortlake tapestry factory, founded in 1619. Indeed, as the ceiling designs are in tempera on paper, it is possible that Clein was here recycling cartoons (preliminary outline drawings) originally intended for tapestries. This is just one example of how decorative ideas can be transmuted between different media.

Ten years later the king had lost his head, and his incomparable collections had been scattered across Europe. In 1660 his son returned as Charles II, determined to restore the old order, but it was to a different world.

The curving, S-scroll decoration appears to have been pressed flat and squeezed into forms that vaguely resemble the human ear

above left: The Green Closet at Ham House in 1886. It is one of the very few surviving Caroline interiors.

right: Van Dyck's portrait of Charles I at Ham still has its original auricular (ear-shaped) frame.

Baroque

The Baroque style originated in Rome in the late sixteenth century and reached its zenith between about 1620 and 1660, the period known as the High Baroque. It sought to unite all the visual arts, using sumptuous decoration and piled-up forms to create spectacular theatrical effects that appealed directly to the emotions. It also embodied the ideas of the Counter-Reformation, the Catholic Church's response to the threat of Protestantism. The style spread rapidly, becoming accepted even in the Protestant regions of northern Europe.

The British response to the Baroque was at first enthusiastic. Charles I commissioned the greatest northern Baroque artist, Peter Paul Rubens, to paint the ceiling of the Banqueting House in Whitehall with an allegory glorifying the monarchy. The king's favourite, the Duke of Buckingham, also had Rubens paint a hardly less modest ceiling to his own glory, a copy of which now hangs above Robert Adam's Neo-classical staircase at Osterley. In 1637 Charles I was sculpted by the supreme genius of the High Baroque, Gian Lorenzo Bernini, but sitter and sculptor never met, and when the king walked to his execution beneath Rubens's Banqueting House ceiling on a winter morning in 1649, British interest in the Baroque seemed to have been cut short equally swiftly.

above: **The sixteenth-century *pietra dura* table-top at Charlecote Park is said to have come from the Palazzo Borghese in Rome, one of that city's greatest Baroque mansions.**
opposite: **The staircase at Powis Castle is animated by Gerard Lanscroon's Baroque murals of 1705.**

One of the few mid-seventeenth-century British sculptors to show any understanding of the Baroque was John Bushnell (c.1630–1701), who studied in Italy in the 1660s and may even have met Bernini. His tomb monuments to the Myddeltons in Chirk church demonstrate what he was capable of, but unfortunately he was as conceited as he was talented; he became impossible to work with and ultimately lapsed into insanity. Among Bushnell's lost works is a bust of the architect William Talman, who in 1698–1704 designed the east range of Dyrham Park in Gloucestershire in a restrained English version of the Baroque style.

Baroque decoration gives the impression of defying gravity. It is perhaps best represented in Britain by the 'flying' canopies of state beds like that at Belton; and by the best of Grinling Gibbons's fruitwood carvings, which seem to float in mid-air (his later sculpture in stone is depressingly earthbound). For the same reason, it was often applied to staircases, which lend themselves particularly well to dramatic spatial effects. On the staircases at Petworth, Powis Castle and Hanbury Hall in Worcestershire illusionistic murals dissolve the space still further.

The most successful muralists active in the late seventeenth century were the French Louis Laguerre and the Italian Antonio Verrio, but neither they, nor their British-born imitator James Thornhill, who decorated the staircase at Hanbury, were of the same calibre as Rubens. Alexander Pope neatly summed up their work in just four lines:

On painted ceilings you devoutly stare
Where sprawl the Saints of Verrio *and*
   Laguerre,
On gilded clouds in fair expansion lie,
And bring all Paradise before your Eye.

Apart from the state bed, perhaps the most characteristic piece of Baroque furniture to be found in British country houses is the *pietra dura* cabinet or table. Literally meaning 'hard stone', *pietra dura* was made from a mosaic of colourful gemstones, such as jasper and onyx, principally in the Florentine workshops of the Grand Dukes of Tuscany, which were founded in 1588. The figurative motifs were often quite modest – fruit or flowers – but the interlacing patterns on the great *pietra dura* table slabs at Powis and Charlecote have a true Baroque swagger. The carved-wood stands were often equally grandiose.

The reaction, when it came, was fierce. In the preface to his *Vitruvius Britannicus* (1715), the Palladian architect Colen Campbell dismissed every aspect of the Baroque:

How affected and licentious are the books of Bernini, and Fontana? How wildly extravagant are the Designs of Borromini, who had endeavour'd to debauch mankind with his odd and chimerical Beauties where the Parts are without Proportion, Solids without their true Bearing, Heaps of Materials without Strength, excessive Ornament without grace, and the whole without Symmetry?

Baroque decoration gives the impression of defying gravity

Restoration

When Charles II was restored to the throne in 1660, the antiquary John Evelyn believed that he would usher in a new golden age for the arts in Britain, to rival what Louis XIV was achieving in France (see p.88). When the king died in 1685 Evelyn's verdict was mixed: '[Charles II] loved Planting, building, & brought in a politer way of living, which passed to Luxurie & intollerable expense.'

Evelyn himself had certainly tried to encourage artists, his greatest discovery being the wood-carver Grinling Gibbons (1648–1721). In January 1671, while walking through a poor part of Deptford, he noticed the young craftsman working on a piece that 'for the curiosity of handling, drawing & studious exactnesse, I never in my life had seene before in all my travells'. Evelyn asked the price and was quoted the very high figure of £100, but 'in good earnest the very frame was worth the mony, there being nothing even in nature so tender, & delicate as the flowers & festoones about it'. Amazingly, this carving has survived, in the Library at Dunham Massey in Cheshire, but in comparison with Gibbons's later work, in which his carved flowers and birds seem barely attached to the wall, the frame looks somewhat stiff and unnatural. It consists of four straight bands of tightly marshalled flowers but already reveals Gibbons's skill at undercutting with fine chisels to create separate, three-dimensional forms from solid pieces of limewood.

This was also the great age of floral plasterwork, which bears many similarities to the frame of the Dunham Massey carving. Indeed, at Belton House in Lincolnshire and Sudbury Hall in Derbyshire rich plasterwork ceilings hang above wall-carvings in the style of Gibbons. In the Saloon at Sudbury in 1675 the London plasterers Robert Bradbury and James Pettifer put up an oval frame of flowers and fruit in the centre of the ceiling, which probably inspired the painting of *The Four Seasons* that later filled it. The runs of more repetitive ornament were cast in reusable moulds by assistants working at ground level. Only the more complicated and sculptural single elements, such as coats of arms, figures and sprays of palm leaves, were modelled freehand *in situ* out of lime plaster stiffened with animal hair – a highly skilled, and backbreaking, task. They were usually painted in shades of white, the sculptural quality of the plasterwork being left to speak for itself without benefit of colour. Sir Roger Pratt, architect of the influential early Restoration house of Coleshill in Oxfordshire, which had similar ceilings, described a typical example:

It is generally adorned with some single or double round Guiloche [see p.62], or square one, … and hath a great pendant rose, at the least in all places where the beams cut each other, but besides these, they are many times wrought with foliages as of laurel, oak, or with fruits, trails, husks etc.

above: **The young Grinling Gibbons was discovered while working on this carving of the Crucifixion (now at Dunham Massey).**
far left: **The plaster ceiling of the Drawing Room at Felbrigg (dated 1687) was probably the work of Edward Goudge, one of the finest plasterers of the age.**
left: **The blue damask hangings in the Queen's Antechamber at Ham were put up between 1679 and 1683.**

'... with silent wonder oft have I beheld
Thy artful works by Nature scarce excell'd'

Nahum Tate. 'To Mr Gibbons on His Incomparable Carved Works', 1684

88 Historical Styles and Designers

Mirror glass was used extensively to reflect the candlelight

above: **The suite of giltwood table and candlestands by Pierre Golle at Knole was probably given to the 6th Earl of Dorset by Louis XIV in 1670–71.**

right: **The late seventeenth-century silver furniture in the King's Room at Knole is very similar to the pieces that once filled Louis XIV's palace at Versailles.**

Louis XIV Style

Louis XIV was king of France from 1643 until his death in 1715. During his minority, the dominant figure was Cardinal Mazarin (1602–61), who gave his name to the *bureau Mazarin* – a desk with drawers on either side, which is decorated with Boulle marquetry (there is an example at Felbrigg Hall in Norfolk, illustrated on p.91).

Once Louis had asserted his personal authority in 1661, he used the arts to glorify his regime on an extraordinary scale. According to Saint-Simon, the king had 'an accurate eye for soundness, proportion and symmetry', which he applied to architecture, interior decoration and gardening. In the first half of his reign, the style favoured symmetry, heavy ornament, solemn colours and expensive materials exquisitely fashioned on a grand scale. This combination of the Italian Baroque and French classicism echoed the formality of court life at the king's new palace of Versailles. Something of this rarefied world can still be recaptured in the State Bedroom at Powis Castle, where a bed inspired by that in which the monarch would have received visitors is placed within a niche behind a balustrade that only princes of the royal blood were allowed to cross.

Louis called himself the Sun King and made a cult of light, taking the face of Apollo in a sunburst as his personal symbol. It appears everywhere: on the Savonnerie carpet made for the Long Gallery of the Louvre (now at Waddesdon Manor), on plasterwork ceilings and especially over fireplaces (a source of light as well as of heat). Because much of the ceremony at Versailles took place at night, mirror glass was used extensively to reflect the candlelight, most spectacularly in the vast Gallerie des Glaces. For the same reason, the furniture in this room was made of solid silver. More than 1,200 pieces of this silver furniture had to be melted down in December 1689 to pay for Louis's disastrous European wars.

The fashion for silver furniture was introduced to Britain by Charles II's French mistress, Louise de Kéroualle, who arrived as part of a diplomatic mission from Louis XIV. Her apartments in Whitehall were, according to Evelyn, 'luxuriously furnished, & with ten times the richnesse & glory beyond the Queenes, such massy pieces of Plate, whole Tables, Stands &c. of incredible value &c'. Fire destroyed her rooms in 1691, but contemporary examples of the same quality survive in the King's Bedroom at Knole, which also contains a four-poster bed that is said to have been made about 1673 by Louis XIV's upholsterer, Jean Peyrard. Knole had particularly close links with France in the late seventeenth century. In 1670–71 the 6th Earl of Dorset took part in an embassy to Louis XIV, who is said to have given him the suite of table and candlestands (now in the Cartoon Gallery), with an inlaid pewter and brass top by Pierre Golle, one of Louis's finest designers.

For much of his reign Louis was at war with Britain, but even these conflicts found artistic expression in Brussels tapestries now at Cliveden and battle paintings now at Plas Newydd. Louis's greatest influence on British taste was also the inadvertent result of hostility – the revocation of the Edict of Nantes in 1685. This act of religious intolerance forced thousands of French Protestants (known as Huguenots) to emigrate to England, among them many of the most talented designers and craftsmen in France. Huguenot metalworkers played a leading part in forming the style of William and Mary silver. Greatest of all these Huguenot craftsmen was Jean Tijou, who came to Britain in 1689. The symmetrical, formally scrolling patterns of the Louis XIV style proved particularly well adapted to the wrought-iron gates he designed for Hampton Court Palace and Chatsworth, among other great houses. Tijou's son-in-law, Louis Laguerre, was to popularise another important element of the Louis XIV style, the Baroque mural (see p.85).

Tijou spread his designs through the engravings in his *A New Booke of Drawings* (1693), although by the 1690s their style was already going out of fashion in France. During that decade Louis began to turn away for the ponderousness of his early style towards something more light-hearted. The Rococo (see p.106) was born in the Trianon at Versailles.

André-Charles Boulle (1642–1732)

Boulle was the finest French cabinetmaker (*ébéniste*) active during the reign of Louis XIV, serving as *ébéniste du roi* from 1672, and his furniture came to represent the ultimate in ornament and craftsmanship in the Louis XIV style (see p.89).

Boulle's work is famous for two things: its marquetry and its ormolu mounts. The marquetry design was cut out with a fretsaw from sheets of brass and tortoiseshell, which had been clamped together. This process produced two sets of the pattern – a 'positive' and 'negative' image – which were often applied to paired pieces of furniture or to the insides and outsides of doors. When the light-coloured brass is laid into a background of dark tortoiseshell, it is known as Boulle; when tortoiseshell is set in a brass background, it is called contre-Boulle. The ornament itself usually consisted of elaborate arabesques in the style of Jean Bérain (see p.94). Boulle also made marquetry in exotic woods, which, according to his biographer, Pierre Crozat, depicted 'species of fruit, and of animals, composing pictures of hunting scenes, battles and fashions accompanied with ornaments in the most refined taste, enriched with bronze, to form tables, writing desks, [casks], *armi* [probably wardrobes], monograms, clocks, friezes'. These are much rarer.

The ormolu mounts on Boulle furniture ostensibly had a practical function – to protect the vulnerable corners of the piece from damage – but they soon became an excuse for extravagant ornament. Ormolu (from the French *or moulu*, 'powdered gold') involved fire-gilding a cast-brass body with a gold-mercury amalgam. Chasing (a form of engraving) and burnishing added further subtleties to the surface. The use of mercury made the process extremely dangerous for the gilders and is now illegal in the West, so true ormolu is impossible to replicate. The mounts themselves usually took the form of masks or figures, sometimes based on Old Master drawings and prints, of which Boulle had a superb collection, including designs by Raphael – a *sorgente deliziosa* ('delightful source') of inspiration, as Boulle himself put it. The rest of the piece was usually veneered in ebony so the predominant colours were black and gold.

Despite Boulle's fame and productivity, very few pieces are fully documented as by him. Rare exceptions are a pair of commodes, which were made in 1708–9 for the Grand Trianon at Versailles. An almost identical commode, now in the Carved Room at Petworth, also has a good claim to be his work. Boulle was influential in popularising the commode form (anglicised as the chest of drawers), which replaced the tall chest. It reached only as far as the dado rail and so was easier to integrate with the new forms of wall decoration that were becoming popular. These depended on wallpapers, tapestries, mirrors and paintings to fill the area above the rail.

Boulle's workshop was destroyed by fire in 1720, but the business was continued by his sons, and reproductions and outright fakes continued to be produced throughout the rest of the eighteenth century and the nineteenth century, to satisfy the demands of aristocratic clients such as George IV and the Marquess of Hertford. Typical of the best Boulle Revival work is the rosewood bookcase of *c*.1820 in the Music Room at Tatton Park in Cheshire. It was probably made by Louis Le Gaigneur, who established a 'Boulle Manufactory' in London and supplied similar Boullework furniture to Windsor Castle.

'The most skilful in Paris'

opposite: **An ormolu mount on the Boulle commode at Petworth.**
right: **A pedestal clock, *c*.1700–25, attributed to Boulle at Waddesdon Manor.**
below: **A *bureau Mazarin* at Felbrigg covered with Boulle-style marquetry.**

William and Mary

The Dutch Stadtholder, William of Orange, and his English queen, Mary Stuart, daughter of the deposed James II, reigned as joint sovereigns from 1689 until 1694. The court style of that era was, perhaps not surprisingly, a fusion of Dutch and English tastes. This was mixed with a dash of the exotic and a continuing, if somewhat ambivalent, envy for the grandeur of Louis XIV's France. Just as Louis was compared to Apollo, so William was depicted as the hero Hercules.

Queen Mary had a particular passion for the exotic luxury goods being imported from India and the Far East in increasing quantities by the fledgling East India Company. She encouraged the already current fashion for Chinese and Japanese blue-and-white porcelain, which was copied in Holland and then in England as blue-and-white Delftware. This was meant for display as much as for use and so was formally arranged on and below cabinets, on wall-brackets, in fireplaces and on mantelpieces – particularly on receding shelves over the new triangular corner chimneypieces. This style of chimneypiece had first been introduced by Charles II, to the dismay of John Evelyn, who predicted that 'it will Spoile many noble houses & roomes if followed; it dos onely well in very Small & trifling roomes, but takes from the state of greater'. The fashion was followed but generally restricted to small rooms, as at Ham in Surrey and at Beningbrough Hall in Yorkshire.

William III brought many foreign designers and craftsmen with him to England, including Daniel Marot (see p.94), and he encouraged others, such as the cabinetmaker Gerrit Jensen, who were already settled here. About 1680 Jensen, who anglicised himself as Gerard Johnson, had established his workshop in St Martin's Lane, which became the centre of the London furniture trade. In 1689 he was appointed 'glasse-seller' and cabinetmaker to the Royal Household. Jensen's particular skill was intricate marquetry, a technique introduced to Britain only about 1675, which entailed gluing a jigsaw puzzle of veneers of different coloured woods, ivory or other materials to the carcass of the piece. The skill lay in cutting out the individual pieces that made up the design so that they would fit together perfectly – something that was possible thanks only to the thinness of the new veneers and the new steel blades in the cabinetmaker's fretsaw. Jensen specialised in 'seaweed' marquetry, which gained its name for obvious reasons and which tried to translate into wood the brass and tortoiseshell marquetry that the great French cabinetmaker André-Charles Boulle had made famous (see p.90). For this reason, Jensen was sometimes known as 'the English Boulle'.

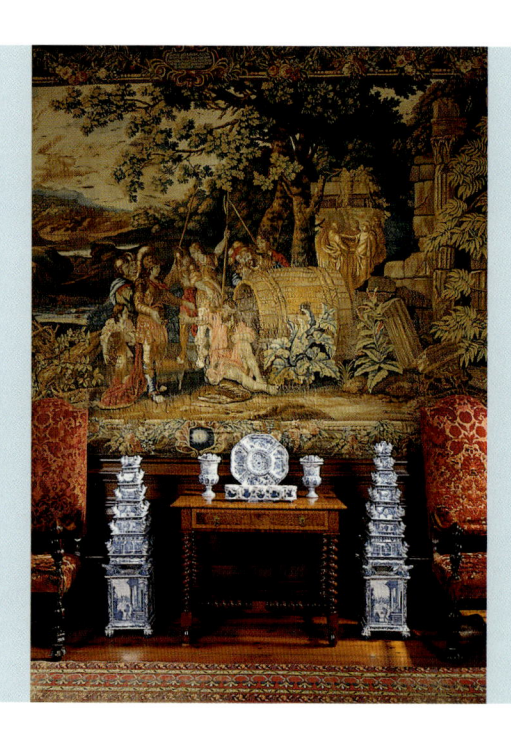

'The Queen brought in the custom of furnishing houses with china-ware'

Daniel Defoe, 1722

left: **Blue-and-white Dutch Delftware pyramid vases in the Diogenes Room at Dyrham Park.**
right: **The technique of marquetry in wood was introduced to Britain only in about 1685. This panel at Charlecote comes from a cabinet probably made about 1690 by the Dutch master Jan van Makeren.**

Daniel Marot
(c.1663–1752)

Marot was the most important of the craftsmen William III brought to England from the Netherlands. He had been trained in the Paris studio of Louis XIV's principal designer, Jean Bérain (1640–1711), and had then probably been employed in the burgeoning royal workshops. However, like many of the finest French craftsmen of the period, he was a Protestant and so was driven out of France when the king re-imposed Catholic orthodoxy in 1685 (see p.89). William took Marot on as the chief designer of the interiors of his new palace at Het Loo near Apeldoorn, and when he became king of England asked him to work on Hampton Court. Between 1689 and 1706 Marot seems to have made regular trips to England.

Marot developed the decorative language of the French court style, which he had learned from his master, Bérain. This derived principally from the grotesque decoration of Raphael's frescoes in the Vatican *Loggie* in Rome (see p.61). Marot's importance lies not in the originality of the motifs he used but in his role as a mastermind supervising every aspect of the decoration of an interior. In this respect, he can perhaps be called the first interior designer. Although he described himself as an architect, he worked in many different media and on many different scales, producing designs for vases, chimneypieces, metalwork, overdoors and doorcases, and especially for upholstery, a trade dominated by the Huguenots at this period.

This was the great age of what became known, slightly later, as the state bed. Its high canopy (or tester), which was often suspended from the ceiling, dominated the bedroom and represented the climax to a sequence of richly decorated rooms. The state bed was frequently the most expensive item of furniture in the house. Traditionally, such canopies were placed over the thrones of monarchs or their representatives to symbolise authority. Decoration was usually concentrated on these canopies and on the headboards below. The state bed at Dyrham Park, which is attributed to the Huguenot upholsterer François Lapierre, has an extremely elaborate tester, consisting of formal scrollwork derived from Marot, and a broken cornice topped by little urns, also indebted to him. Adding greatly to the effect are the applied braids and tassels, known collectively as *passementerie*, which were produced by the Huguenot silk-workers concentrated in Spitalfields in the East End of London. Marot's influence as an integrated designer is also apparent at Dyrham in the matching crimson and yellow velvet upholstery of the chairs, footstools and window pelmets. They stood originally in a room hung with tapestry.

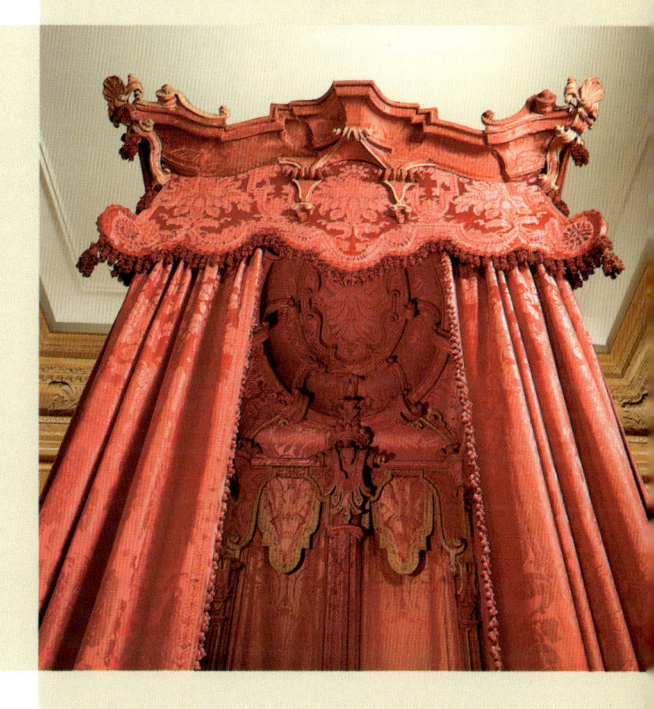

Marot spread his influence through the engravings of his designs, which numbered over 100. Although these were not published as a collection until 1700, they were circulated widely in suites of six during the 1690s and inspired an unusually large amount of surviving decoration, probably because so few other ornament prints in the style were being engraved in Britain in the late seventeenth century. Typical are the carved-wood cornices and overdoors in the principal rooms at Beningbrough Hall, which were the work of William Thornton.

Marot lived to a great age, long enough to witness the dawn of Neo-classicism, but by then his style belonged to the distant past.

above: **The State Bed at Beningbrough Hall is one of the finest surviving examples in the Marot style.**
opposite: **The carved wood cornice in the Drawing Room at Beningbrough Hall was probably based on published engravings of Marot's designs.**

He can perhaps be called the first interior designer

96 Historical Styles and Designers

Elegant proportions were considered more important than ornament

right: **The chapel plate at Dunham Massey was supplied by Isaac Liger between 1706 and 1717.**
far right: **The panelled Dining Room at Canons Ashby was created by Edward Dryden about 1710.**

Queen Anne

Queen Anne's reign (1702–14) witnessed a gradual move from the showy Baroque style favoured by the courts of the Restoration and William and Mary periods towards a quieter classicism. The great exception to this generalisation was Vanbrugh's Baroque Blenheim Palace in Oxfordshire, but even its owner, Sarah, Duchess of Marlborough, who fell out spectacularly with her architect, ruefully admitted that she preferred 'to have things plain and clean, from a piece of wainscot to a lady's face'.

The change can be seen in the furniture and silver commissioned by George Booth, 2nd Earl of Warrington (1675–1758), who inherited Dunham Massey in Cheshire in 1694. He began by buying silver wine fountains and walnut benches carved with ornate scrollwork, both in the Baroque style of Daniel Marot, but moved on to prefer plain walnut chests with simple curved legs and ebony beading and silver decorated with no more than his engraved coat of arms. The new spirit is apparent in his chapel: the panelling is bare apart from the Corinthian pilasters that flank the altar, on which sits a gilt communion dish against a Spitalfields silk reredos. Elegant proportions were considered more important than ornament to create the right effect, as Edward Dryden realised when he came to create a new dining room at Canons Ashby in Northamptonshire about 1710. To make room for his new panelling, which was articulated by Corinthian pilasters, he took the drastic step of raising the ceiling and lowering the floor.

Queen Anne was too worn out by her efforts to produce an heir to inspire a sparkling court, and, indeed, the new style had little to do with her circle. Thanks to the lapsing of the Licensing Act in 1695, publishing was booming, and journals such as Addison and Steele's *The Spectator*, which appeared daily in 1711–12, preached the gospel of simplicity and gentility to a growing 'polite society' with the money to spend on leisure and luxuries. Mompesson House, built in 1701 in the cathedral close of Salisbury, can stand for the many thousands of comfortable country and town houses put up during this period for the gentry: a commonsense plan, well-proportioned rooms, large sash-windows and plain moulded panelling made it easy to adapt to changing ways of living and changing taste (Rococo plasterwork was added to Mompesson in the 1740s). So the houses of this era survived and inspired the Queen Anne Revival of the late nineteenth century.

The Assembly Rooms at Bath functioned like a cultural stock exchange

Georgian

The word Georgian traditionally describes the era of the Hanoverian dynasty, from the accession of George I in 1714 to the death of George IV in 1830. As a stylistic label, however, it is particularly unsatisfactory. George I and II contributed little to the visual culture of their age, while the greatest royal patron of the early Georgian period, Frederick, Prince of Wales, never became king and was never awarded the 'Frederickian' style label that his efforts deserved. However, the greatest royal patron of the late Georgian era, George IV, did receive that accolade; 'Regency' is considered on p.136.

Although the classical style predominated in Georgian interiors, it could take many forms and be combined with non-classical styles. The era embraced, among others, Palladianism, Rococo, Gothick, Chinoiserie, Neo-classicism, Greek Revival and Regency. If one wants to define a 'Georgian attitude' to interior decoration, one has to look beyond the specific labels at broader social trends.

The eighteenth century was a period of huge economic expansion and growth in the luxury trades that provided the essential furnishing for Georgian 'polite society' – clothing, ceramics, furniture, glass, silver and works of art. All of these were brought together in the archetypal building of the era, the Assembly Rooms at Bath, which functioned like a cultural stock exchange. Here people could come to show off the latest fashions by dancing and pass on the latest trends by gossiping.

This exchange of ideas encouraged in some a longing for elegance and calm solemnity, which was summed up in the classical Roman ideal. So, for instance, it led to Lord Cobham being commemorated in the guise of a Roman general on top of a column at Stowe; a Latin inscription at the bottom credits him with 'a more elegant notion of gardening, first revealed in these grounds'. For the same reason Sir John Dutton, 2nd Baronet, of Sherborne in Gloucestershire was memorialised in 1749 by Michael Rysbrack (1694–1770) in the toga and sandals of a Roman senator, leaning nonchalantly on a classical urn and with his legs crossed – the mark of masculine suavity in the mid-eighteenth century.

The energy and self-confidence of the Georgian era affected others very differently. It provoked in them only a sense of conflict and disgust, which was expressed most memorably in the social satires of Hogarth and the caricatures of Gillray and Cruikshank. Their protagonists often express the crudest of human passions within the most elegant of Georgian interiors. It is a reminder, if one were ever needed, of the dangers of trying to divine the 'spirit of an age' too strictly from the style of its architecture.

opposite, far left: **The epitome of Georgian male elegance: Rysbrack's monument to Sir John Dutton, 2nd Baronet, in Sherborne church.**
opposite, left: **The Ballroom at the Assembly Rooms in Bath.**
above: **Rumbustuousness confronts elegance in William Hogarth's** *The Country Dance* **from his** *The Analysis of Beauty* **(1753).**

Palladianism

This style takes its name from the north Italian architect Andrea Palladio (1508–80). Inigo Jones first introduced the style to Britain in the early seventeenth century, and it was revived by Lord Burlington and his circle a hundred years later, when it rapidly became the preferred style for the new country houses of the ruling class.

From his studies of Roman architecture Palladio had devised an interpretation of the classical style that was dignified, humane and flexible. He also spread the word by publishing his designs in the influential *Four Books of Architecture* – a lesson learned by his British followers. The style depended heavily on a mathematical system of proportion. So, for instance, Stourhead House, one of the first eighteenth-century English country houses in the Palladian style, was laid out around a 30-feet-cube entrance hall, flanked by a music room and cabinet room that were both 20 feet by 30 feet.

Palladio himself gave little guidance on how to decorate the interiors of his houses, but this did not stop his British followers from trying to devise a Palladian style of interior. Their solution tended to be primarily architectural in character – indeed, to look like an external façade turned inside out. Horace Walpole criticised the Palladian architect and designer William Kent for this: 'His chimney-pieces, though lighter than those of Inigo [Jones], whom he imitated, are frequently heavy; and his constant introduction of pediments and the members of architecture over doors, and within rooms, was disproportionate and cumbrous.' Perhaps for this reason, many country houses that are Palladian on the outside have lighter, Rococo-style interiors.

Giacomo Leoni (c.1686–1746) was a Venetian architect who would have known Palladio's buildings at first hand. He came to Britain in 1682–3 specifically to study Inigo Jones's Palladian revival work, and in 1715–20 published the first complete English translation of Palladio's *Four Books*, which at once became a key source for the Palladian movement. The 2nd Lord Onslow was a political rival of Sir Robert Walpole, who was not only the dominant politician of the age but also the creator of Palladian Houghton Hall in Norfolk. It is unsurprising, therefore, that when, in the early 1730s, Onslow decided to build a new country house at Clandon Park in Surrey, he should have chosen the Palladian style and turned to Leoni.

Large entrance halls lend themselves to an architectural treatment in the Palladian style, and the Marble Hall at Clandon is one of the most spectacular Palladian spaces in Britain. The vast marble chimneypieces use the full vocabulary of the style: a chunky egg-and-dart moulding frames the fireplace; scrolled brackets support the mantelpiece, the frieze of which centres on a mask; the overmantel contains a relief of a classical sacrifice (a common subject in Palladian houses) carved by Michael Rysbrack, the favourite sculptor of Walpole at Houghton and of Henry Hoare at Stourhead; it is set within a so-called 'Kent frame', which can be recognised by its projecting corners and heavy moulding; and topping all this is a broken pediment.

above: **The Saloon ceiling at Uppark, which is in the style of the Palladian architect James Paine. The central oval is especially Palladian.**
opposite: **One of Leoni's Palladian chimneypieces in the Marble Hall at Clandon Park.**

The style depended heavily on a mathematical system of proportion

102 Historical Styles and Designers

The first British architect to take a serious interest in furniture

William Kent
(1685–1748)

Kent was the most talented exponent of the Palladian style (see p.100). He began as a painter. In 1709 he set out for Italy with John Talman, the son of the architect of Dyrham, and spent the next ten years there studying the great fresco cycles of the Baroque. Kent received a prestigious commission to decorate Kensington Palace, but despite his training he remained an indifferent mural painter. Fortunately, while in Italy, he was also 'continually a-drawing ornements & Architecture … things yt I think will be necessary for use in England'. Lord Burlington, the *éminence grise* of the Palladian movement, encouraged him to turn towards architecture and interior and garden design. Kent was keen to oust the Baroque taste – 'that Dam'd Gusto that's been for this sixty years past,' as he put it – but he was equally suspicious of the newly fashionable French Rococo style: 'It is just the same in Painting as ye French Musick is most ungratefull to ye Ears, so is there painting to ye Eyes.' He turned instead to the example of the first British Palladian, Inigo Jones, and in 1744 John Vardy bracketed the two men when he published *Some Designs of Mr Inigo Jones and Mr William Kent*.

Palladio is not known to have produced furniture, but this did not stop Kent (the first British architect to take a serious interest in furniture) from designing pieces in the style. For Inigo Jones's Double Cube Room at Wilton, the most influential Palladian interior in Britain, he probably designed a suite of settees, which are, as one would expect, architectural in style. The seat is supported by hefty scrolled brackets at the corners and sphinxes with tails that turn into acanthus scrolls. Good, early copies of these settees sit in the Ionic Temple at Rievaulx Terrace in Yorkshire. Even more solid are the benches supplied in 1731 by James Moore the Younger for the Great Room at Lodge Park in Gloucestershire, another Palladian double cube. They follow very closely a Kent design published in Vardy's 1744 book, with a characteristically Kentian scrolled pediment and scallop shell on the back. Shells also appear on the silver chandeliers that Kent designed for George II in the mid-1730s, together with other favourite Kent motifs: sphinxes, acanthus leaves, lion's masks and cornucopia. Two from the set now hang in the Library at Anglesey Abbey in Cambridgeshire.

Documented furniture by Kent is relatively rare, but his influence was huge, as Horace Walpole noted:

Kent's style … predominated authoritatively during his life; and his oracle was so much consulted by all who affected taste that nothing was thought complete without his assistance.

opposite: **A bench made for Lodge Park in 1731 to a design by William Kent.**

below: **A silver chandelier at Anglesey Abbey, designed by Kent for George II in the mid-1730s.**

Gothick

This was the first phase of the Gothic Revival, spanning the period from about 1740 to about 1780. It was inspired by the architecture of the Middle Ages, particularly in its final, Perpendicular form. In fact, the Gothic style never entirely disappeared, surviving in buildings like Staunton Harold church in Leicestershire, which was built in 1653 in defiance of the Commonwealth.

Gothick was driven by a sense of romance and fantasy rather than by the concern for archaeological correctness that characterised the Victorian phase of the Gothic Revival (see p.152). The spindly tracery and elongated shafts of much Gothick decoration give it a rather flimsy appearance; indeed, the most famous Gothick building, William Beckford's Fonthill Abbey in Wiltshire, was so poorly built that its tower collapsed in 1825.

Using Gothick often had patriotic and political motives, as it was identified with a Saxon world that predated the Norman invaders and was thought to be distinctively English and free. For this reason, the Gothic Temple at Stowe, designed by James Gibbs and begun in 1741, was known as the Temple of Liberty when it was first built. In his *Gothic Architecture Improved* (1747) Batty Langley recommended the 'Saxon' style (as he called it) as suitable 'for all parts of private buildings; and especially in Rooms of State, Dining Rooms, Parlours, Stair-cases, &c'. The fashion caught on to such an extent that William Whitehead could write in 1753: 'A few years ago everything was Gothic: our houses, our beds, our bookcases, and our couches, were all copied from some parts or other of our old cathedrals.'

Gothick designers venerated the surviving remnants of the medieval past, responding particularly strongly to romantic Gothic ruins seen by moonlight, and none more so than the gentleman-architect Sanderson Miller (1716–80), who completed the turrets on Gibbs's Gothic Temple and designed several new garden buildings at Wimpole and elsewhere as readymade Gothic ruins. In 1754–5 he advised John Ivory Talbot on his new Entrance Hall at Lacock Abbey in Wiltshire, in which Gothick niches and a statue of the foundress of the original Augustinian nunnery recall the place's medieval past.

The most influential advocate of Gothick was Horace Walpole, author of the first Gothick novel, *The Castle of Otranto* (1764) and creator of the most complete example of the style, Strawberry Hill. Walpole attracted a circle of like-minded antiquaries, known as the Committee of Taste, who included John Chute of The Vyne in Hampshire. Chute is thought to have designed the Gothick fireplace and possibly the fan-vaulted canopies and ceiling of the Gallery at Strawberry Hill. In the Tudor Gothic chapel of his own home he installed illusionistic wall-paintings that conjured up an even more perfectly Gothic space of intersecting vaults and spandrels. Another Walpole accomplice, Richard Edgcumbe, had inherited a still more ancient and untouched place, Cotehele in Cornwall. He furnished Cotehele, not to live in, but to show off to visitors as a romantic medieval survival (see p.35). Edgcumbe therefore installed a number of ebony turned chairs, which Walpole and his circle believed were genuine Tudor relics. The chairs turned out to be seventeenth-century and not even English, but that was typical of Gothick's somewhat shaky scholarship.

James Wyatt, the architect of Fonthill, kept the Gothick spirit alive well into the early nineteenth century, when his approach came under increasing attack. His first Gothick mansion was Sheffield Park in Sussex; one of his last was Plas Newydd on the Isle of Anglesey, where in 1805–9 his assistant, Joseph Potter, who was cathedral architect at Lichfield, designed a Gothick chapel. The space is now occupied by Rex Whistler's Dining Room mural. This is appropriate, as Whistler was one of the most convincing revivers of the Gothick style.

left: **The ebony chairs at Cotehele were once thought to be Tudor.**
opposite: **A Gothick fantasy by a member of the Pether family at Anglesea Abbey.**

105

Rococo

Rococo was the dominant style in France, northern Italy, southern Germany and central Europe during the first half of the eighteenth century. It marked a playful interlude between the drama of the Baroque and the severity of Neo-classicism.

The word Rococo came into use only in the 1790s as a term of abuse, when the style was already dead, and appears in English for the first time only in 1822. It sounds Italian, but in fact derives from the French *rocaille*, meaning the shells and water-worn rocks used to line shell-rooms and grottoes, which were a favourite Rococo creation. The little shell-house in Hatfield Forest in Essex is typical. It was constructed in the 1750s, probably by the young daughter of the family, Lavinia Houblon. Young women, who preferred lighter colours and much gold and white, were key patrons and consumers of the Rococo style, which fostered a mood of fantasy, pleasure and relaxation. In form, the decoration resembles the inside of a conch shell: fluid, asymmetrical, with many curling C- and S-scrolls, and a sense of tottering excess. It is seen at its most extreme in engraved cartouches and carved picture and mirror frames, which

left: Matthias Lock's Rococo designs for mirror frames probably inspired Luke Lightfoot's carvings in the North Hall at Claydon (opposite).

provoked the wrath of the Abbé le Blanc, whose *Letters on the English and French Nations* were translated into English in 1747:

They heap cornices, bases, columns, cascades, rushes and rocks, in a confused manner, one upon another; and in some corner of this chaos, they will place a cupid in a great fright, and have a festoon of flowers above the whole.

The style was introduced to Britain in the early eighteenth century by *émigré* artists, who congregated in the St Martin's Lane area of London and met to exchange ideas at Slaughter's coffee-house. Many were French, including Philippe Mercier, who painted the Belton conversation-piece in 1724–6. The Rococo conversation-piece distilled the new informality in family life with particular charm. There was also a more enlightened attitude towards animals and the natural world, and scenes from the animal fables of Aesop and La Fontaine became increasingly popular subjects for Rococo decoration.

In Britain Rococo decoration was considered too light-hearted to be used outside, apart from for heraldic cartouches and garden buildings. More sober Palladian remained the preferred style. Inside, it was a different story, and the style was much employed in smaller rooms used by women, particularly for ceiling plasterwork. The best continental plasterers (or *stuccadores*) came from the Ticino, a small, Italian-speaking region of southern Switzerland. They included the Lafranchini brothers, who were responsible for the superb Rococo decoration in the Saloon and Dining Room at Wallington in Northumberland. The most skilful English craftsmen in plaster working outside London were the interrelated Yorkshire families of the Perritts and the Roses. Thomas Perritt (1710–59) and his apprentice, Joseph Rose the Elder (c.1723–80), provided Rococo ceilings for James Paine's Palladian Nostell Priory in Yorkshire in the 1740s. Perritt's brother William went on to make the even more exuberant Rococo decoration at Farnborough Hall in Warwickshire in 1750, which, like that at Wallington, incorporates oval wall-mirrors that add to the sense of movement. The Dublin group of plasterers achieved still higher standards, which can be appreciated in their work at Florence Court in Co. Fermanagh.

Rococo decoration reached its climax in England in the North Hall at Claydon House in Buckinghamshire, where the extraordinary niches, overmantel and door cresting were created in the 1760s by the mysterious carver, Luke Lightfoot, who also designed interiors at Claydon in the closely related Gothick and Chinoiserie styles (see pp.104,114). Sir Thomas Robinson wrote in 1769: 'Mr Lightfoot's design for furnishing the great Eating Room [now the North Hall] shock'd me so much and is so much the ridicule of all who have seen or heard of it that it will indeed be what he expressed very justly – such a Work as the World never saw.'

Thanks to Robinson, Lightfoot was sacked from the job and never found another as ambitious, so Claydon remained a one-off.

Lightfoot's patron, Lord Verney, was one of the backers of the Ranelagh pleasure gardens in London, which, with its rival, Vauxhall Gardens, did much to encourage Rococo artists and embodied the Rococo love of pleasure. Two of Francis Hayman's decorative paintings for the supper-boxes at Vauxhall Gardens survive at Sizergh Castle in Cumbria.

The rise of Rococo coincided with the European discovery in 1709 of how to make porcelain on a commercial scale. The Meissen factory jealously guarded the secret of hard-paste porcelain, which gave its famous figurines an unmatched crispness and delicacy, but French and English makers tried to produce something similar in soft-paste. Among the most charmingly Rococo is the Chelsea factory's *The Music Lesson*, which was based on a painting by the ultimate Rococo artist, François Boucher, and incorporates a Rococo scrolled base.

For the Rococo Revival, see p.142.

Fluid, asymmetrical, with many curling C- and S-scrolls, and a sense of tottering excess

left: **William Perritt's Rococo plasterwork in the Dining Room at Farnborough Hall.**
right: **A Rococo silver cup of the 1740s at Anglesey Abbey.**

Louis XV Style

The term denotes the French version of the Rococo (see p.106), which flourished during the first half of Louis XV's reign, from 1715 to about 1750. The new style reflected a relaxation in the formal etiquette of the French aristocracy, which had been heralded by Louis XIV himself, when he commented: 'Il faut qu'il y ait de la jeunesse mêlée dans ce que l'on fera' ('There should be youthfulness in what we do'). It also responded to the growing influence of French women, who wanted smaller tables (*bonheurs du jour*), at which to write and sew, and wider *bergère* armchairs, which would accommodate their fuller skirts. The most powerful was the king's mistress, Madame de Pompadour, who was an important patron of the Vincennes porcelain factory.

The first phase of the Louis XV style – sometimes known as the *Régence*, after the regency of the king's cousin, Philippe, duc d'Orléans (1715–23) – is epitomised by the furniture of Charles Cressent (1685–1758). Cressent developed the Louis XV form of the commode, with its serpentine front, tall legs, plain wood veneers and highly sculptural ormolu mounts (he had started out as a sculptor), which often entirely masked the drawers; indeed, these commodes were really an extension of the wall decoration rather than functional pieces of furniture. Such was Cressent's fame that much has been attributed to him on shaky evidence; one of the very few authentic works, made about 1730, now stands against French Rococo panelling of the same date in the Grey Drawing Room at Waddesdon Manor in Buckinghamshire.

Cressent often worked with the designer Nicolas Pineau (1684–1754), who helped to invent the *genre pittoresque*, the second and most light-hearted phase of the Louis XV style. The hedonistic fantasies of the painter François Boucher are perhaps its ultimate expression. About 1731 Pineau carved luxuriant gilt pier-glasses for the Hôtel de Villars in Paris, which incorporate paintings within the wildly scrolled and asymmetrical upper

opposite: **The triumph of the serpentine line. Charles Cressent's commode of *c.*1730 at Waddesdon Manor.**

Cressent developed the Louis XV
form of the commode

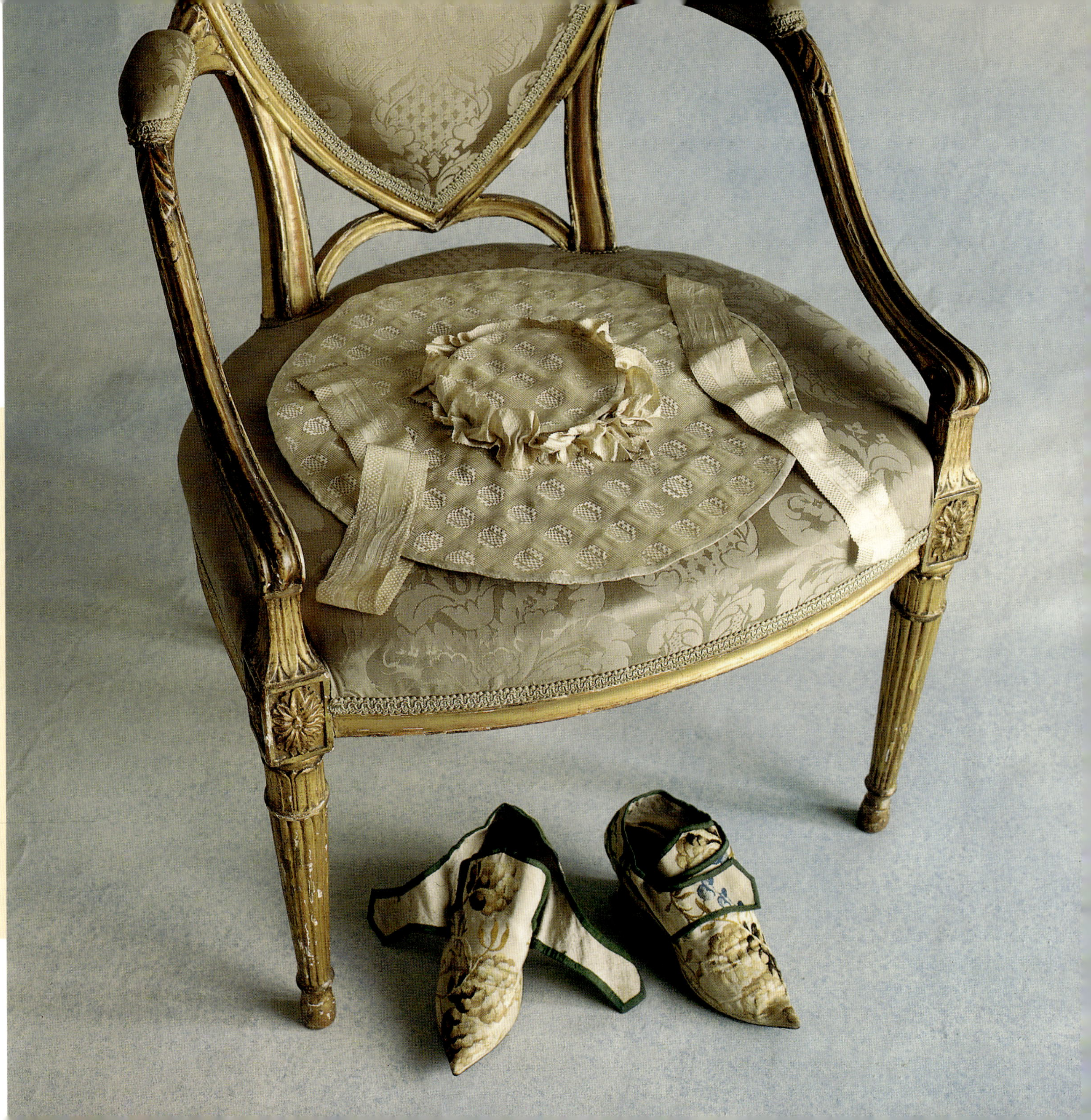

element of the frame. They are now installed in the Dining Room at Waddesdon.

Rococo designers tried to integrate every element of an interior, an effect that can be partly recaptured in the French Dining Room at Cliveden in Buckinghamshire, where Pineau's decoration for the small salon of the château d'Asnières was reconstructed in 1897. Large sheets of mirror glass abound, as light and glitter were crucial to the Rococo effect, and they are integrated with the fireplace and the *boiseries* (carved wall-panelling), to achieve a total ensemble. The carving is gilded, as it was originally – something unusual for a French country house in the eighteenth century. The room dates from 1750–51, at the end of Pineau's career, and although it still deploys the Rococo language of fluid C- and S-scrolls, the total effect is more sober and symmetrical, foreshadowing the onset of Neo-classicism, which dominated the final years of Louis XV's reign.

opposite: **'The typical Louis XV chair was the *bergère*, which came into existence about 1725, a large, deep, embracing armchair into which the sitter could only sink in a way which would not have conformed to social conventions two decades earlier' (Sir Francis Watson).**
below: **The French Dining Room at Cliveden incorporates panelling by Nicolas Pineau from the château d'Asnières.**

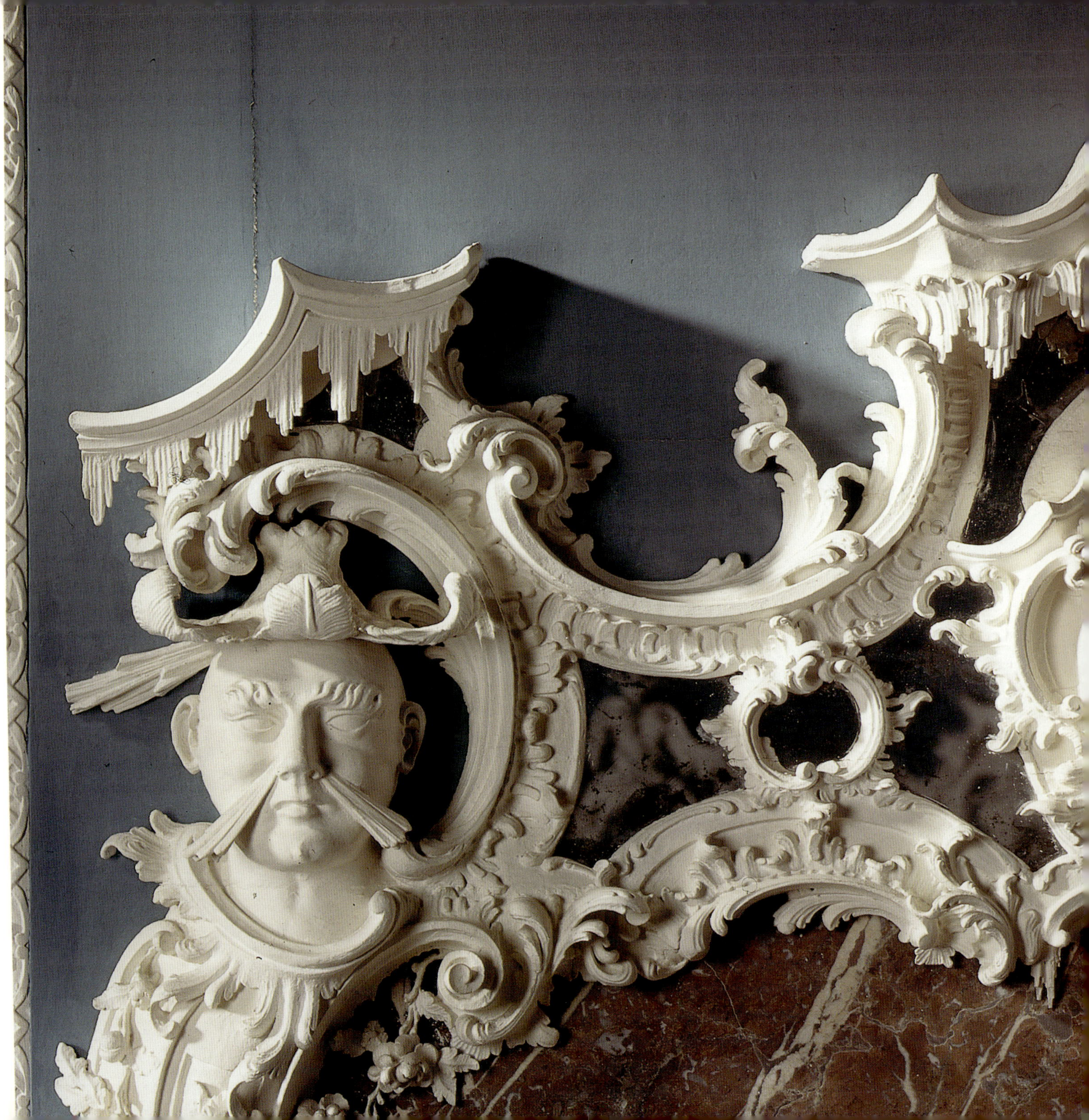

Chinoiserie

In the 1830s Charlotte Bedingfeld of Oxburgh Hall in Norfolk was working as a lady-in-waiting at the Brighton Pavilion, which has the most elaborate Chinoiserie, or Chinese-style, interior ever created in Britain: 'A seemingly enchanted palace, the Pavilion can neither be described nor guessed at, it is the dream of some Chinese Poet (if there be such a thing).' Western reactions to Chinese art have often combined bafflement with fascination. The motifs were exotic – dragons, pagodas and lotuses, jagged mountains and gnarled trees – and so were the materials – lacquer, silk, chintz and, above all, porcelain. But that only added to the spell cast by the far-off dream world of 'Cathay' on Western designers who sought to appropriate and imitate it.

China has meant china since at least the fifteenth century, when the first blue-and-white porcelain started arriving in the West. By the early seventeenth century Dutch and Portuguese merchants were importing 'Kraak' porcelain in huge quantities. Much of it was made specifically for the Western market, retaining traditional Chinese motifs but copying European shapes. In turn, the Dutch potteries at Delft produced replicas in earthenware. At the end of the seventeenth century Queen Mary led the 'chinamania', which saw tall blue-and-white vases being displayed in symmetrical patterns on corner chimneypieces, tallboys and wall-brackets. The effect can still be admired at Ham House in Surrey and Beningbrough Hall in Yorkshire.

left: **Mustachioed Chinamen animate the chimneypieces in the Chinese Room at Claydon.**

The fashion for entire Chinoiserie interiors reached its height in the early 1750s at the same time as the Rococo style (see p.106), with which it shared a love of the playful, exotic and asymmetrical. (Sir William Temple coined the pseudo-Chinese term *Sharawadgi* for this 'beauty of studied irregularity'.) It was in decline by 1757 when Sir William Chambers published his *Designs of Chinese Buildings, Furniture, Dresses, Machines, and Utensils*, which proved influential, even though he expressed 'no wish to promote a taste so much inferior to the antique and so very unfit for our climate'.

In the same year the idiosyncratic designer Luke Lightfoot (see p.108) was employed to transform Claydon House in Buckinghamshire, where the Chinese Room remains one of the more bizarre explorations of the Chinoiserie taste in Britain. Moustachioed Chinamen support pagoda-like doorcases, while the Chinese tea ceremony is played out in plaster within an alcove decorated like a Chinese fretwork tea-house and above a divan on which the family themselves would doubtless have taken tea. China had been associated with tea since the earliest times, when Chinese porcelain had been shipped to Europe in tea-chests.

Chambers recommended the Chinese style for bedrooms, so it is perhaps not surprising that the furniture-maker Thomas Chippendale opted for it in 1765 when he was commissioned to redecorate the State Bedchamber at Nostell Priory in Yorkshire. He designed not only a new suite of green lacquer furniture decorated with Chinese landscapes and figures but also the Chinoiserie mirror, whose frame features the mythical ho-ho bird and a Chinese pagoda complete with a fretwork fence of a pattern often found on the backs of 'Chinese Chippendale' chairs. Chippendale also supplied the painted Chinese wallpaper, which had been made for the Western market since the mid-seventeenth century and is found in several country-house bedrooms. It usually featured exotic birds (as here) or town views with scenes of daily life, or a combination of the two. Confusingly, it was known at the time as 'India paper' because it had first been imported by the East India Company.

The Chinoiserie interior quickly fell from favour with the coming of serious, symmetrical Neo-classicism (see p.120) in the late eighteenth century. However, the style was revived during the Regency and Victorian periods, particularly for garden buildings, with which it had been associated since the time of Chambers. One compartment of the mid-Victorian garden at Biddulph Grange in Staffordshire was named 'China', as it brings to life all the elements of the willow-pattern plate. This pattern is the most ubiquitous example of the Chinoiserie taste: it draws on genuine Chinese elements but was fixed only in the late eighteenth century by Staffordshire potters and adapted so that it could be mass-produced by transfer-printing on to white earthenware.

'On ev'ry shelf a Joss divinely stares,
Nymphs laid on chintzes sprawl upon our chairs;
While o'er our cabinets Confucius nods,
Midst porcelain elephants and China gods.'

James Cawthorn, *Of Taste*, 1756

right: **Thomas Chippendale's State Bedchamber at Nostell Priory** combines many aspects of Chinoiserie taste: green lacquer furniture; a mirror frame carved with a pagoda and ho-ho birds; and Chinese painted wallpaper and porcelain.

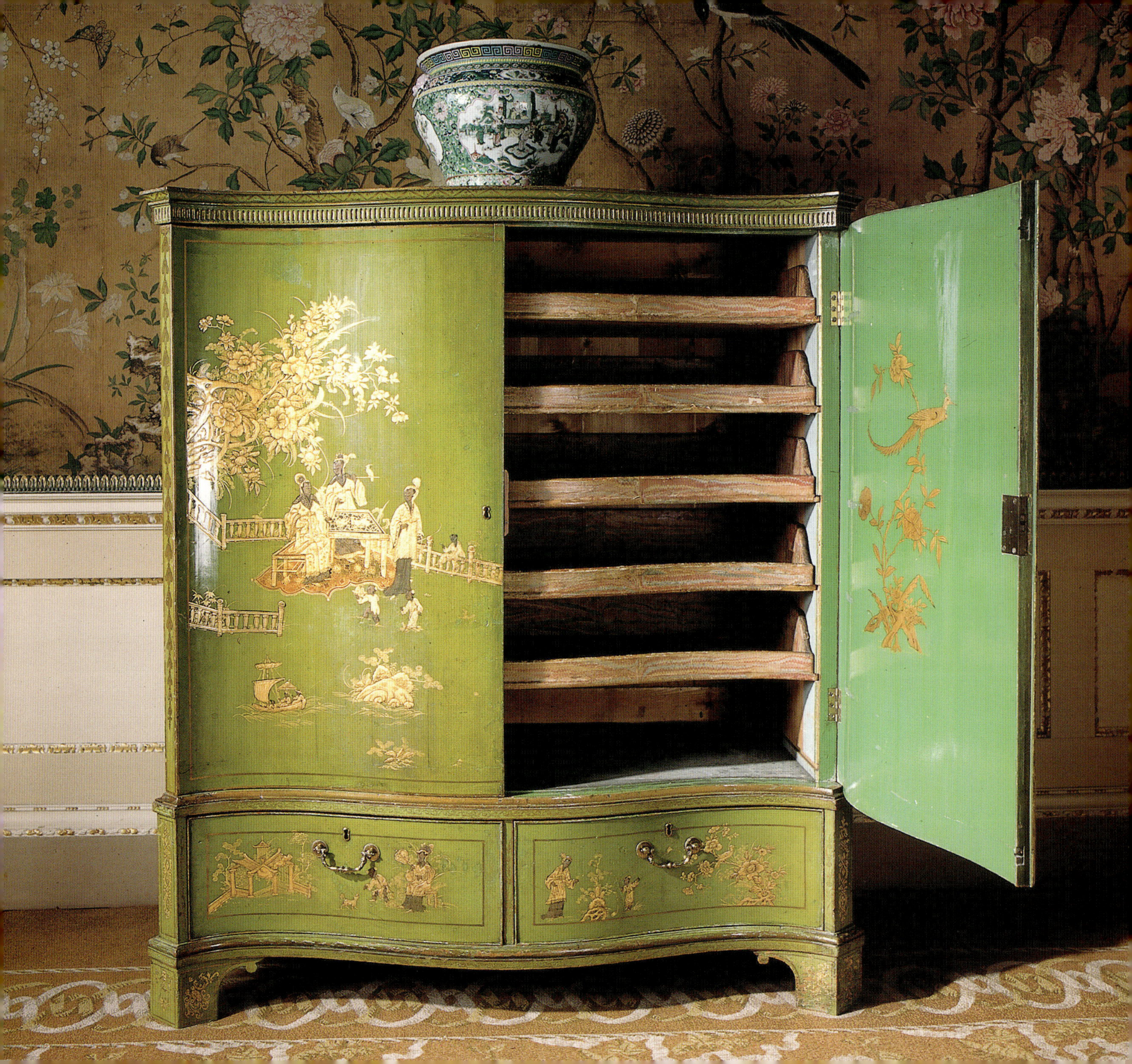

Thomas Chippendale
(1718–79)

Thomas Chippendale was the most famous and influential of all English cabinetmakers. The son of a joiner, he was born in Otley in Yorkshire, and although he was well established in London by the age of 30, he still depended on Yorkshire patrons such as Sir Rowland Winn of Nostell Priory for many of his most important commissions.

Chippendale's importance rests less on the pieces he actually made than on *The Gentleman & Cabinet Maker's Director*, the first edition of which he published in 1754. It was so successful that it was reprinted in 1755 and revised in 1762. Illustrated with 161 plates, this was the first comprehensive English book of furniture designs, providing ideas for every kind of piece – from the grandest to the most mundane – that might be required in a smart new house. The designs were mainly in the Rococo style (what Chippendale called 'the modern taste'), which had been developed by a group of artists working in a small area of London around St Martin's Lane, where Chippendale himself had his workshops. The *Director* also advertised pieces in the related Gothic (see p.104) and Chinese styles, and the 'Chinese Chippendale' style, with its distinctive latticework friezes and chairbacks, became closely associated with him (see p.116).

The first comprehensive English book of furniture designs

But Chippendale was never dogmatic about style. He produced pieces in the Palladian style, such as the mahogany library desk at Nostell Priory, which was already somewhat old-fashioned by the time it was delivered in 1766. At Nostell he also worked in the new Neo-classical style, having probably been recommended to Sir Rowland by its chief exponent, Robert Adam (see p.124), who trusted Chippendale to provide furniture that would suit his interiors. Chippendale offered Sir Rowland a complete design service, supplying wallpapers, decorative fillets and pelmets as well as furniture for some rooms. However, he was never on the same gentlemanly terms as Adam with his patron, and their correspondence degenerated into arguments about late payment and undelivered items.

Among the 310 subscribers to the first edition of the *Director* were no fewer than 169 craftsmen working in various branches of the furniture trade, and Chippendale seems to have been unconcerned when they began enthusiastically copying his designs. In the preface to the *Director* Chippendale claimed to have himself made every item illustrated, but very little of the surviving furniture that is based on the *Director* designs actually originated in his workshop. 'Chippendale style' soon came to have a life of its own, spawning variants in, for instance, faraway Philadelphia.

The business was carried on by his son, Thomas Chippendale the Younger (1749–1822), who supplied a suite of library furniture in the Egyptian style and a vast picture frame with a ram's-head crest for Sir Richard Colt Hoare at Stourhead in 1802. When the younger Thomas went bankrupt in 1804, Colt Hoare helped to get him back on his feet.

above: **Chippendale's library desk in the Palladian style for Nostell Priory.**
opposite: **The green lacquer chinoiserie chest of drawers from the Chippendale suite in the State Bedchamber at Nostell.**

Neo-classicism

The style developed, apparently independently, in both Britain and France in the 1750s and continued to dominate taste, particularly in sculpture, well into the nineteenth century.

This 'new classicism' advocated a more rigorous interpretation of classical forms, based on first-hand study of Roman (and, slightly later, Greek) architecture, sculpture, pottery and decoration. A broad international movement, it embraced both the Greek Revival and the Pompeian and Etruscan styles (see pp.132 and 134) and spread throughout Europe and its colonies.

The most successful early exponent of Neo-classicism in Britain was Robert Adam (see p.124), who developed a vocabulary for the decoration of Neo-classical interiors that most of his rivals felt obliged to adopt. Indeed, in his *Works in Architecture* (1773–9), Adam complained about unnamed rivals who were stealing his ideas. Walpole immediately pointed the finger at James Wyatt (1746–1813), who may have got to know Adam's work through his brother, Samuel, who had been clerk of works for Adam at Kedleston. Wyatt used many of the same motifs, but in a slightly sparer fashion, and increasingly ate into Adam's country-house market in the 1780s.

Perhaps the most original Neo-classical designer of Wyatt's generation was Henry Holland (1745–1806). Unlike Adam, Holland never toured the Roman remains of Italy, and he did not visit France until the 1780s, but he seems to have studied the most advanced French treatises on classical architecture at an early age. He also employed a French assistant and a team of highly skilled French craftsmen who understood Neo-classical ornament. From 1771 Holland went into partnership with his future father-in-law, the great landscape architect, 'Capability' Brown, with whom he worked at Claremont in Surrey. The exterior is conventional – indeed, by then somewhat old-fashioned – Palladian, but the interior, although never finished, shows a sophisticated use of space and restrained ornament that is essentially Neo-classical. Holland was never as ruthlessly ambitious as Adam, but from the late 1770s he was taken up by the Whig aristocracy and received the plum commission of his generation, for the building and decoration of the Prince Regent's Carlton House.

left: **George Steuart's design for the Outer Library at Attingham Park.**
right: **James Wyatt's 1778 design for the Library ceiling at Belton.**

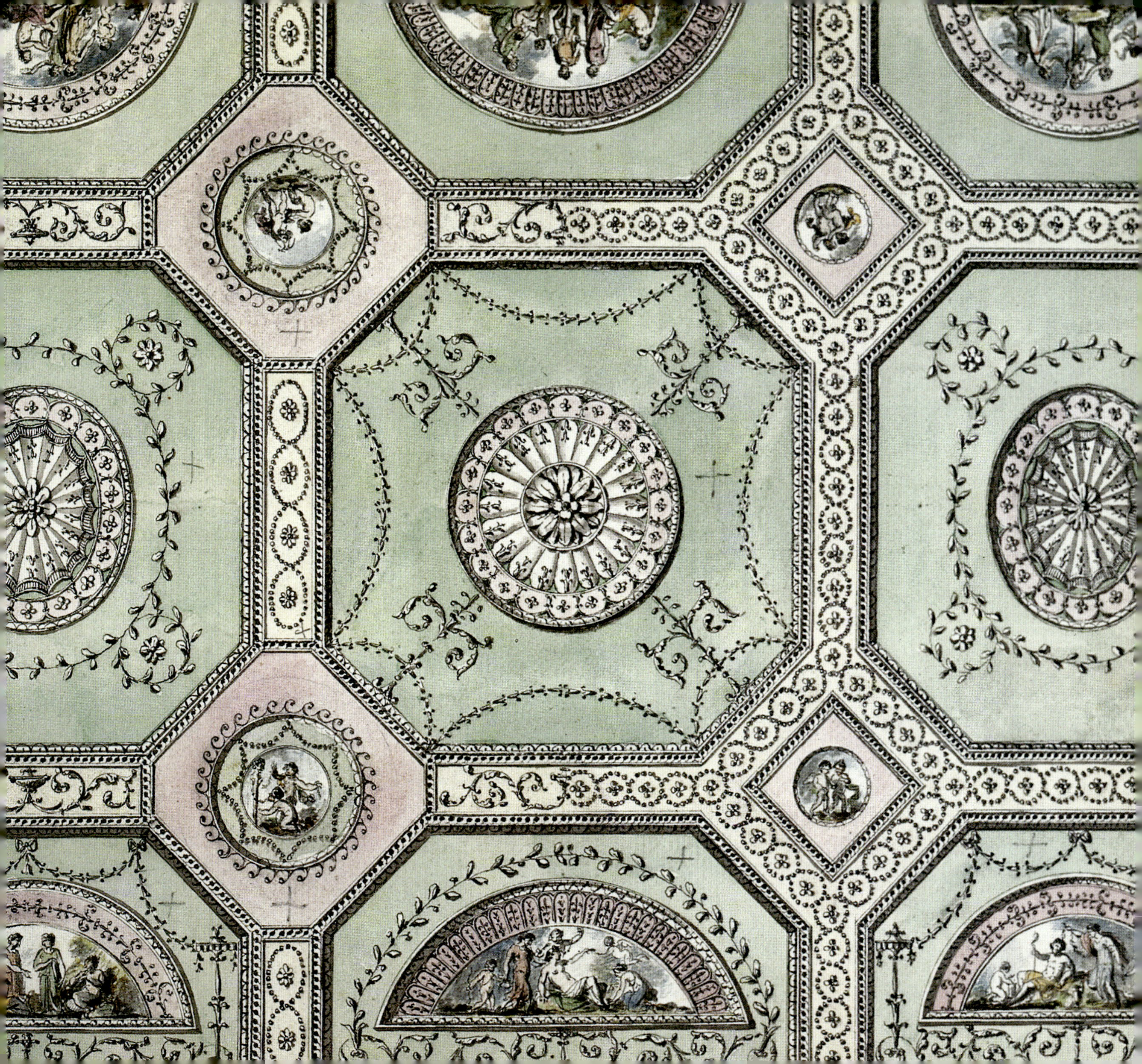

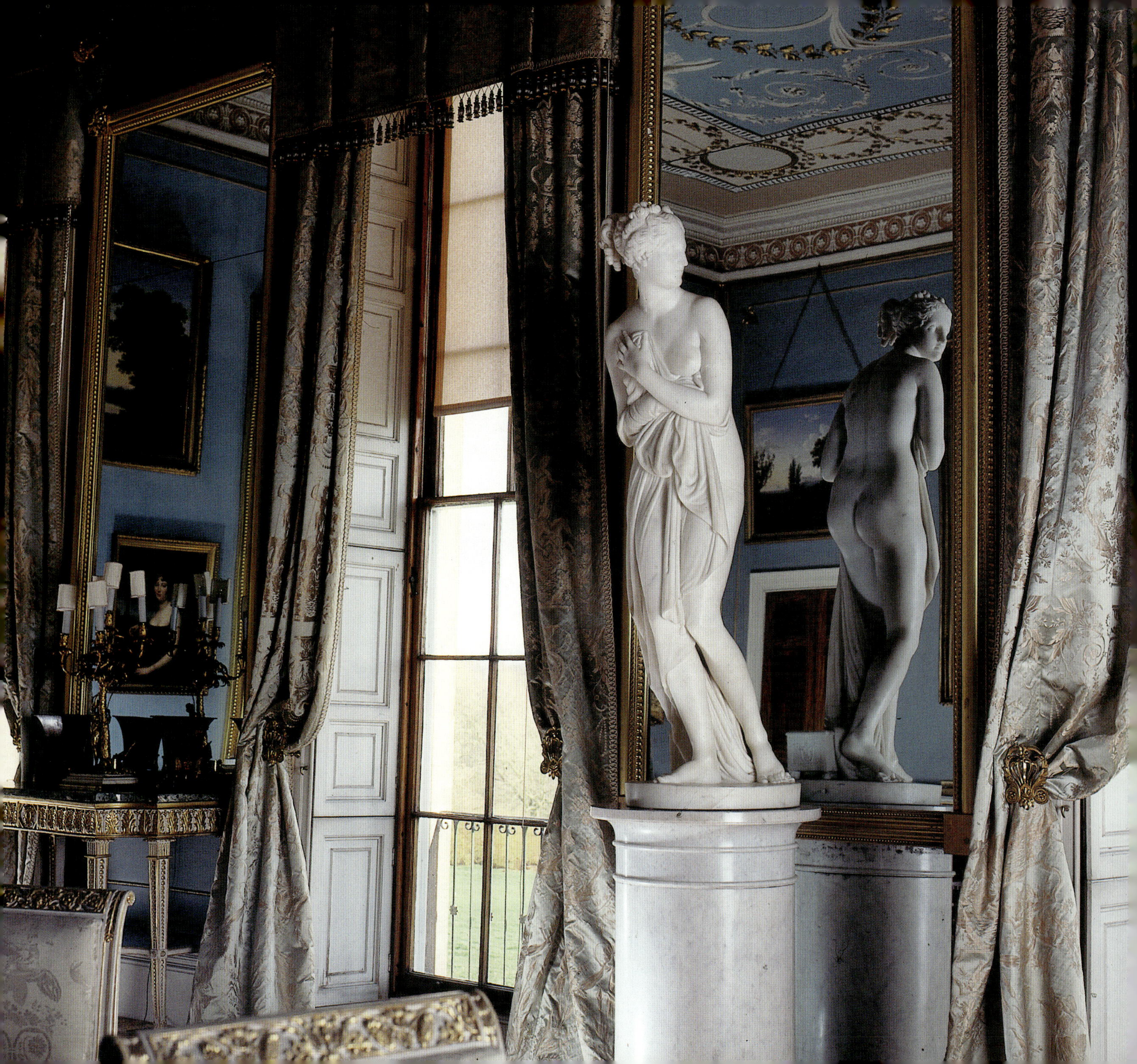

'Such as the great of yore, Canova is today'

Lord Byron

left: Canova's *Venus Italica* in the Drawing Room at Attingham Park. The poet Heine dreamed of making love to this statue.
right: The Staircase Hall at Berrington Hall.

Holland's Berrington Hall (1778–81) may be in then remote Herefordshire, but it shows his craftsmen working to the highest London and Paris standards. The Marble Hall immediately sets the tone: the ceiling looks at first like a saucer dome but is actually a flat circle, carried on corner spandrels, which create the illusion. The marble floor echoes the ceiling in the Adam manner. The corner overdoors, which break into the frieze above, are filled with the trophies of arms found in many entrance halls, but from them hang swags of husks – a typical Holland touch taken from French Neo-classicism.

Most of the doors are there for symmetry rather than use. George Steuart (*c.*1730–1806), the architect of Attingham Park (1783–5), which is in neighbouring Shropshire, may have studied with Holland. The columns of the portico certainly have the same typically Neo-classical, stretched proportions as those at Berrington. Steuart's finest Neo-classical interior is the Outer Library, with its dramatic giant order of fluted Ionic pilasters, breaking a Greek key frieze. In the 1790s the 2nd Lord Berwick decided to convert the room into a sculpture gallery. Sculpture was one of the most revered survivals of classical antiquity, and there were few Neo-classical interiors that did not have some sculptural decoration. Lord Berwick commissioned a copy of the Apollo Belvedere to stand in this room with his collection of Etruscan vases. He also got Robert Fagan to decorate the empty panels above the bookcases with grisaille paintings of classical statues, such as the *Castor and Pollux*. The statuary and the vases have been sold, but the 8th Lord Berwick found a worthy replacement when he bought a version of the *Venus Italica* by the greatest of all Neo-classical sculptors, Antonio Canova. His influence ensured that Neo-classical remained the preferred style for ideal sculpture in Britain until at least the mid-nineteenth century.

Among those who studied with Canova in Rome was James Wyatt's great-nephew, Richard James Wyatt, sculptor of the monumental *Flora and Zephyr* (1834) at Nostell Priory. Canova even left his mark on the Library chimneypiece at Ickworth in Suffolk, which incorporates small copies of his *Eros and Psyche* and *Bacchus and Ariadne* groups, probably acquired in Rome by the Earl-Bishop of Bristol. This is, however, something of an oddity, as Neo-classical chimneypieces were usually plainer and less sculptural than their Palladian predecessors.

Robert Adam
(1728–92)

Between the 1760s and 1780s Adam developed his own delicate version of the Neo-classical style. He was given little opportunity to create whole buildings from scratch, but his interiors became so fashionable that he gave his name to a style – a rare achievement for a British designer.

Adam began his career working in his father's architectural practice in Edinburgh, but he was ambitious to succeed in London. To this end, he decided in 1754 to spend five years studying the monuments of classical antiquity in Italy. Here he also made useful contacts with potential patrons on the Grand Tour and became friendly with the designer G.B. Piranesi, whose use of classical ornament and forms offered 'the greatest fund for inspiring and instilling invention in any lover of architecture that can be imagined'.

The germ of the Adam style was already apparent in 1759 in his decorations for Hatchlands Park in Surrey, his first major project after returning from Italy. Particularly innovative were the wall-panels decorated with grotesque ornament of thick acanthus scrolling around urns, although he found it difficult to get the English craftsmen to give up 'their angly Stiff Sharp Manner'. By the mid-1760s he had achieved his mature style, at Kedleston Hall, Osterley Park and Nostell Priory, among many other country houses. By 1773, when he published the first volume of his *Works in Architecture*, he could justly claim to have brought about 'in the decoration of the inside, an almost total change'. He had discredited Palladianism as a style for interior decoration: 'The massive entablature, the ponderous compartment ceiling, the tabernacle [Kent] frame, almost the only species of ornament formerly known, in this country, are now universally exploded.' Adam replaced the linear succession of rectangular boxes that comprised the early Georgian apartment with an altogether more intriguing series of spaces, articulated with semicircular niches and oval ante-rooms: the domed ceilings of the baths of Domitian and Caracalla in Rome were a particular inspiration. He decorated these with the full range of Neo-classical ornament – griffins, sphinxes, urns, anthemions, putti, swags – applied with an almost Rococo lightness and sense of rhythm. The patterns became increasingly flat, complex and attenuated but were dismissed by Walpole as 'all gingerbread, filigraine, and fan-painting'.

Adam planned every element of the room from the carpet to the ceiling (which were often made to correspond) and down to the handles on the doors. His aim was 'elegance, gayity, & variety', which can be seen most clearly in his ceilings. Of the 650 Adam ceiling designs preserved in Sir John Soane's Museum, only five are identical. Variety was also achieved through colour, which was concentrated on the ceiling. He disliked the old fashion for uncoloured plasterwork, preferring the backgrounds to be 'coloured with various tints to take off the crudity of the white'.

opposite: **The ceiling of the Etruscan Dressing Room at Osterley Park.**

'Elegance, gayity, & variety'

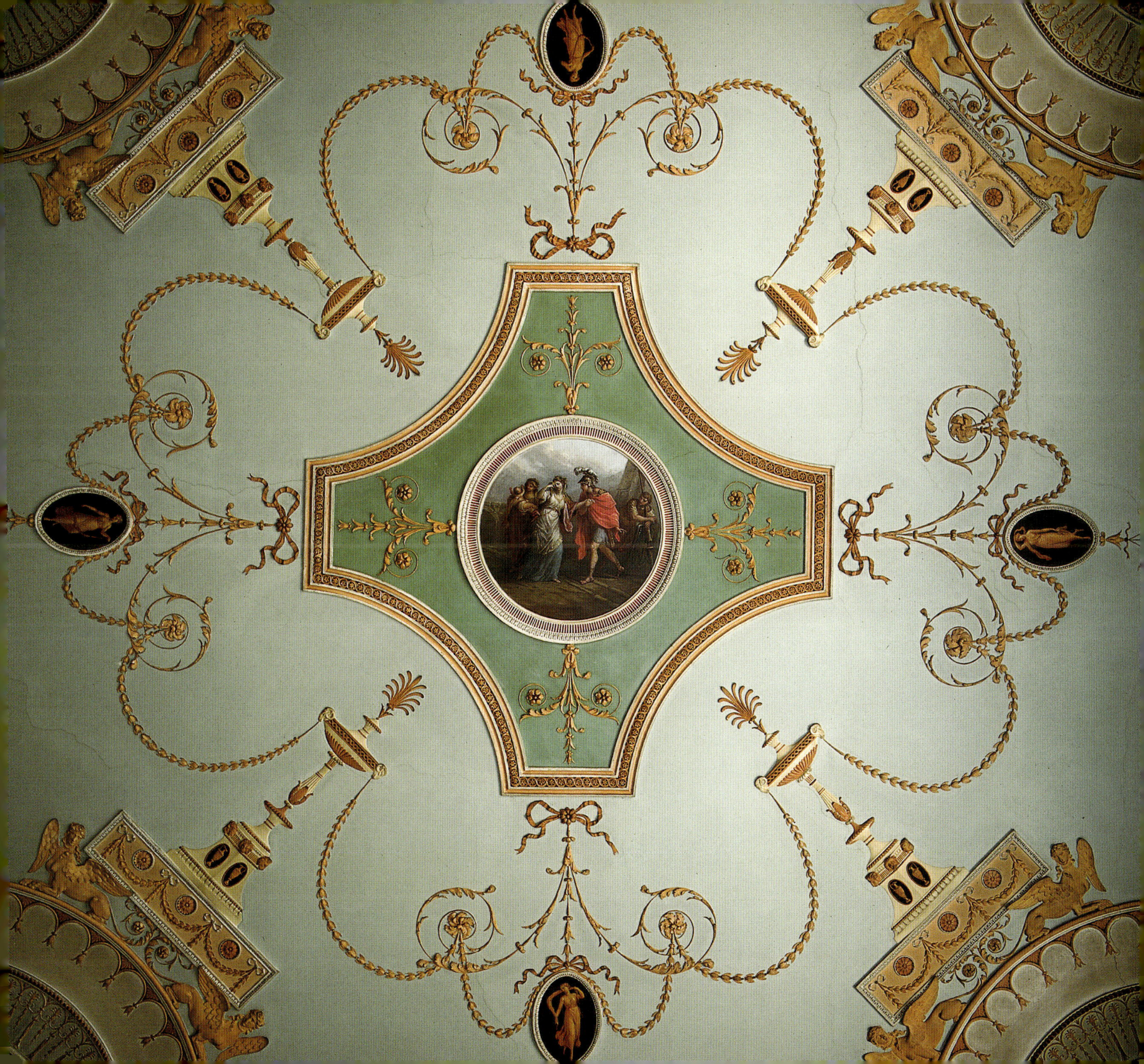

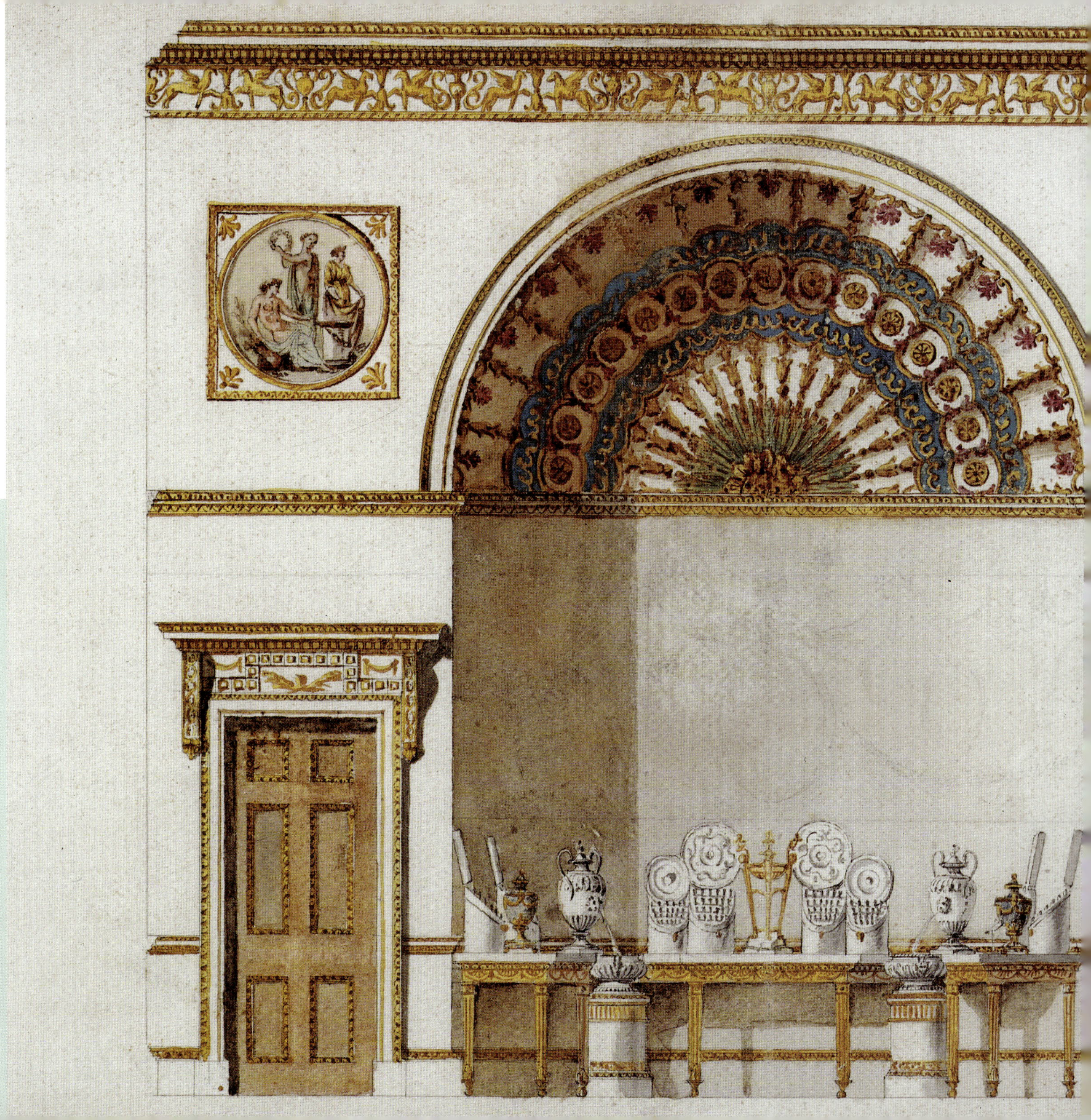

'The Great Parlour in the best taste of all'

Horace Walpole, 1768

Pea green and pale mauve are the shades most often associated with the Adam style, although his designs proposed a much wider and more robust range of colours.

Adam was productive and successful thanks largely to the group of craftsmen he relied on to carry out his designs, principally G.B. Cipriani and Antonio Zucchi for painted wall decorations, and Joseph Rose the Younger for plasterwork. He often recommended Thomas Chippendale to supply furniture for his interiors (as at Nostell Priory) but seems not to have produced designs for Chippendale. Adam himself designed mainly wall furniture that would integrate with his interiors, such as the semicircular sideboard that sits in the Dining Room alcove at Kedleston. With its narrow, tall and straight legs and simple frieze front, this is one of the first pieces of British Neo-classical furniture. The sideboard form itself is said to have been Adam's invention.

Adam's designs for urns were often translated into silver, particularly as racing cups, for which there was an increasing demand in the late eighteenth century. The main body of the piece was usually left plain, with Neo-classical decoration concentrated on the handles, neck and foot.

left: **Adam's design for the Dining Room (Great Parlour) alcove at Kedleston, which was created to display Lord Scarsdale's finest pieces of silver.**

Louis XVI Style

Louis XVI came to the throne of France in 1774, but the style associated with his name was popular from the mid-eighteenth century. It was essentially Neo-classical, marking a reaction against the Rococo and a partial return to the Louis XIV style (see p.89).

The hallmarks of the style are symmetry, restraint and rectilinear forms, combined with a greater and more accurate use of classical motifs: Vitruvian scroll, anthemion and palmette, and Greek key. Chair legs became straight and tapered; cabinets lost their serpentine curves and became flat-fronted and upright. This was the great age of French cabinet-making, although many of the best craftsmen working in Paris, such as Jean-Henri Riesener, Martin Carlin and Jean-François Oeben, actually came from Germany. Typical of the new style is the secretaire commissioned from Riesener by Marie-Antoinette in 1777 for Louis XVI's own use in the Petit Trianon, their private retreat at Versailles. The ormolu mounts on this straight-sided desk are comparatively modest and make no attempt to disguise its various elements, as Cressent might have done (see p.110). The marquetry in the upper panel, which drops down to form the writing surface, depicts a woman personifying silence in a simple oval frame, flanked by ribbons and swags.

The gilt frieze above is a plain acanthus scroll. Many of the best Louis XVI pieces were decorated with plaques of Sèvres porcelain, such as another, rather smaller secretaire at Waddesdon, which was made, also in 1777, by Carlin. Again, there is much use of ribbon swags, a type of ornament that Carlin particularly favoured.

Cabinetmakers such as Pierre Langlois brought the Louis XVI style to Britain. He was established in London by 1759–60, and soon became a serious rival for the best native craftsmen. His commodes, made in the 1760s, in the Saloon at West Wycombe in Buckinghamshire show his mastery of Louis XVI-style marquetry, here applied to a carcass that still follows the more old-fashioned serpentine form of the Louis XV commode.

Another French arrival was the decorative painter Louis André Delabrière, who had worked at Bagatelle, the villa near Paris belonging to Louis XVI's brother, and went on to decorate Carlton House for the Prince Regent. He is thought also to have worked at Attingham Park in Shropshire on the painted decoration of the Boudoir – a French word for a new French form of room – which combines a pared-down Neo-classical interpretation of the Raphael grotesque with thin *rinceaux* (scrolls). The white marble chimneypiece in this exquisite little room is also in the Louis XVI style.

The Sèvres factory dominated the production of high-quality porcelain in France during this period. The business belonged to the king, who allowed no other French factory to use gilding or coloured backgrounds on their porcelain and ensured that his courtiers supported the business. His own most important commission – indeed the most lavish commission of the century – was the so-called *Grand Service de Versailles*. Work began in 1783 and was due to take 23 years to complete, so high was the standard of figure painting demanded. In the event, the French Revolution intervened. The pair of wine coolers, dated 1791 and 1792 and now at Upton House in Warwickshire, were among the final pieces delivered, when the king and his family were already under arrest, but he still found time to record their arrival. In 1793 Louis XVI was executed and the royal cipher was removed from Sèvres wares, but the simple shapes and the Neo-classical subjects of the Versailles service continued to influence the taste of the new regime.

opposite: **The secretaire was designed by Riesener in 1777 for Louis XVI's own use in the Petit Trianon at Versailles.**
right: **The Boudoir at Attingham Park.**

Boudoir – a French word for a new French form of room

Greek Revival

left: **'Athenian' Stuart's reconstruction of the tripod from the Choragic Monument of Lysicrates in his *Antiquities of Athens*. Copies were made for Kedleston and Shugborough.**
opposite: **Flaxman's Shield of Achilles at Anglesey Abbey.**

The Greek Revival was one element within the broader Neo-classical movement. It grew out of the belief that ancient Greece had produced the purest forms of classical architecture, which could be understood only by accurately recording the surviving monuments.

The birth of the Greek Revival in Britain is traditionally dated to 1762, when James Stuart and Nicholas Revett published the first volume of *The Antiquities of Athens*. Even before then, however, their researches had inspired a replica of the Athenian Tower of the Winds at West Wycombe. Among the subscribers was Thomas Anson, who in the 1760s commissioned 'Athenian' Stuart (as he was soon nicknamed) to reproduce the monuments recorded in his book as garden buildings in the park at Shugborough in Staffordshire. On a much smaller scale, Stuart designed a perfume-burner for the Kedleston dining room, based on his reconstruction in the *Antiquities* of the tripod once thought to have topped the Choragic Monument of Lysicrates in Athens. The tripod was a quintessential Greek Revival form, which inspired a gilt stand decorated with rams' heads at Shugborough, also designed by Stuart.

The first volume of the *Antiquities* did not illustrate any of the major monuments of the Athenian Acropolis, and Stuart was so indolent that he never got round to publishing them (the task was left to his widow in 1789). However, it was soon possible to study the real thing in London, thanks to the Earl of Elgin, who in 1799 had set out to acquire 'examples in the actual object, of each thing, and architectural ornament – of each cornice, each frieze, each capital … as much as possible'. In 1807 he put on public display the 'Elgin Marbles', the sculptural decoration he had removed from the frieze and pediments of the Parthenon. His aim was to encourage 'the progress of taste in England', and although some connoisseurs, including Richard Payne Knight, were dismissive, most artists were ecstatic. Humphry Repton sent his son, John Adey, to sketch the sculpture and reproduced a section of it in 1813 as stained glass in the Servery at Uppark in Sussex. The fashion for all things Greek stretched from women's chignon hairstyles and muslin dresses to *klismos* chairs.

The sculptor John Flaxman (1755–1826) was one of the first to enthuse about the Elgin Marbles. He had made his name designing urns derived from Sir William Hamilton's famous collection of Greek vases (see p.134). His outline illustrations for Homer's *Odyssey* and *Iliad* (published in 1794) were much admired by Thomas Hope, who became a patron of him and of the Greek Revival, combining the two in the Flaxman Room at his London house. Flaxman was invited to restore the Elgin Marbles, but refused, arguing that they were more valuable

The fashion for all things Greek stretched from women's chignon hairstyles and muslin dresses to *klismos* chairs

untouched. This was a key moment in taste, when respect for the battered, but original, fragment replaced concern for a smoothly restored whole, which had hitherto been the Neo-classical ideal. It is why the so-called 'Headless Lady' (a fragment similar in style to the Parthenon frieze) was preserved in this state at Felbrigg. Thomas Legh of Lyme Park brought back similar pieces from Athens in 1812.

Flaxman was the finest British designer of Greek Revival silver. His masterpiece was the silver-gilt Shield of Achilles, which was inspired by the long description in the *Iliad* of the shield made for the Greek hero by the divine blacksmith Hephaistos. Flaxman worked on the project for over ten years in collaboration with the royal goldsmiths, Rundell, Bridge & Rundell, who displayed the first copy at the lavish Coronation Banquet for George IV in 1821.

132 Historical Styles and Designers

Pompeian

The Pompeian style was inspired by the Roman wall-paintings that were discovered in the mid-eighteenth century, when archaeologists excavated the cities of Herculaneum and Pompeii, which had been buried by the eruption of Mount Vesuvius in AD 79.

What emerged were spectacularly colourful schemes: animals and nymphs (the so-called 'Herculaneum dancers') disported themselves within an architectural framework of trellises and candelabra grotesques (see p.61), on a deep red background. Designers had already realised that red was a good colour on which to hang gold-framed pictures, and 'Pompeian Red' soon became the preferred shade for picture gallery walls. The discoveries at Pompeii were to influence not just the colour of walls, but textiles, ceramics and painted furniture, and among the first British designers to make use of Pompeian motifs was 'Athenian' Stuart in his drawings for Kedleston in 1757.

The term was often loosely applied. One of the earliest complete interiors in the style, the Pompeian Gallery at Great Packington in Warwickshire, which was designed by Joseph Bonomi in 1785–8, was not, in fact, based on the Pompeian murals but on decorations in the Baths of Titus in Rome.

The same was true of the Pompeian Room at Ickworth in Suffolk, created a hundred years later. The west wing had been left unfinished on the death of the Earl-Bishop of Bristol in 1803 and was still an empty shell in 1876, when the 3rd Marquess's architect, F.C. Penrose, suggested decorating the vaulted New Room 'in the Pompeian manner'. The scheme was based on Roman murals that had been discovered in the Villa Negroni on the Esquiline Hill in Rome in 1777. The Earl-Bishop had bought the detached frescoes to decorate Downhill, Co. Londonderry, but they seem never to have reached Ireland. Fortunately, they were recorded in thirteen hand-coloured engravings, which veiled the figures' genitals but seem otherwise to have been faithful to the original's bright red, purple, blue and yellow shades. J.D. Crace (see p.158) interpreted the scheme in more muted tones – terracotta, yellow and light buff, with sky blue above the cornice – which were skilfully arranged to lead the eye upwards and articulate the complex space. It all fulfilled Crace's belief that 'we have, in colour, a handmaiden to Architecture capable of most grateful service'. The female figures on the end walls were based on the famous Herculaneum dancers, but the other scenes derive directly from the Negroni decoration. The panels are framed by narrow borders and divided by very thin 'candelabra' columns on black backgrounds. Griffins, anthemions and Greek key friezes abound. Crace also designed black ebonised bookcases to fit the alcoves.

> Red was a good colour on which to hang gold-framed pictures

opposite: **The Pompeian Room at Ickworth.**

Etruscan

Among the British visitors most fascinated by the excavations at Herculaneum and Pompeii was Sir William Hamilton (1730–1803), ambassador to the court of Naples (and long-suffering husband of Nelson's mistress, Emma). Hamilton put together a huge collection of recently excavated ancient vases, of which he published a catalogue in four handsome volumes from 1766. He believed that these vases, decorated with reddish-brown and white figures on a black background, had been produced by the Etruscans, the ancient inhabitants of Etruria (modern-day Tuscany), who had lost out to the Romans in the struggle for central Italy. (The vases were, in fact, Greek.)

Hamilton's book caused a sensation, inspiring a brief craze for Etruscan-style interiors. The first seems to have been the tea-room in the Prospect House at Wimpole Hall in Cambridgeshire, which was decorated with 'Etruscan figures in colours' about 1766 by 'Athenian' Stuart. With typical self-aggrandisement, Robert Adam claimed to have invented the Etruscan style; 'We have not been able to discover, either in our researches into antiquity, or the works of modern artists, any idea of applying this taste to the decoration of apartments.' Adam designed no fewer than eight Etruscan rooms, the most complete surviving example being the Etruscan Dressing Room at Osterley Park in Middlesex. He adopted the terracotta red and black colours of Hamilton's 'Etruscan' vases for the painted figures in this room, but otherwise they bear little relation to the originals, and the rest of the ornament was borrowed from a quite different source – Roman and Renaissance grotesques (see p.61). Adam himself devised the sky-blue background.

Even more influential in spreading the Etruscan taste was the potter Josiah Wedgwood, who in 1768 named his new Staffordshire factory Etruria in honour of his Etruscan forerunners. From 1769 Wedgwood was producing tablets and medallions decorated with 'Etruscan red burnt-in grounds', which were marketed as suitable for 'inlaying ... in the Pannels of Rooms and Chimneypieces, or for hanging up as ornaments in libraries ... or as Pictures for Dressing Rooms'. When Horace Walpole saw the Etruscan Dressing Room in 1778 he at once made the connection, describing it as being 'painted all over like Wedgwood's ware. ... It is like going out of a palace into a potter's field.' Wedgwood went on to produce vases that echoed both the

With typical self-aggrandisement, Robert Adam claimed to have invented the Etruscan style

colours and the shapes of the antique originals. In 1786 Hamilton paid tribute to his role: 'A Wedgwood and a Bentley [his business partner] were necessary to diffuse that taste so universally, and it is to their liberal way of thinking & … acting that so good a taste prevails at present in Great Britain.'

The fashion for Etruscan interiors had died out by 1790, but the passion for collecting ancient vases lived on. At Sudbury Hall in Derbyshire you can still see the remains of the famous collection made by the 5th Lord Vernon, who himself masterminded pioneering excavations of Etruscan tombs at Cumae in central Italy in the mid-nineteenth century. In this way he acquired a beautiful Etruscan necklace and numerous vases, which he displayed on the bookcases that once lined the Long Gallery at Sudbury Hall.

opposite: **An 'Etruscan' red figure vase at Powis Castle.**

right: **The Etruscan Dressing Room at Osterley Park.**

Regency

Strictly speaking, the term covers only the years 1811–20, when the Prince of Wales (later George IV) served as Regent, but in the decorative arts it usually describes the period from the 1790s to 1830, when the prince was an influential patron.

Although Britain was at war with France for much of this period, the prevailing influence remained French Neo-classicism; some British aristocrats, such as the 3rd Earl of Egremont, even created shrines to Napoleon. However, it was an eclectic era, when numerous other styles were revived: Tudor Gothic, Restoration, Louis XIV, Grecian, Egyptian, Rococo, Indian, Chinese. What was newer was the emphasis on archaeological correctness. Among the upper classes furniture became more solid and more ostentatious but was moved away from the walls and arranged with greater informality, reflecting a more relaxed way of life. In 1820 Sir Henry Bedingfeld visited the Residenz in Weimar and was distressed to find the old ways still being followed: 'chairs all round the room and no tables, a disposition of things calculated to render an assembly formal and one's entry into a room a little appalling.'

Picturesque effects out of doors were matched by a new theatricality in interior decoration, expressed most completely in the panoramic sweep of French scenic wallpapers. Henry Holland designed not only Sheridan's Theatre Royal, Drury Lane, but also the interiors of the Prince Regent's Carlton House, the greatest town house of the Regency era. Nash's terraces and Wyatville's Windsor Castle were scene-painting in stucco.

Carlton House has long since disappeared, but something of its splendour can still be glimpsed at Castle Coole in Co. Fermanagh, which was refurnished with grand Regency pieces in 1807–24 by the Dublin upholsterers John and Nathaniel Preston for the 2nd Earl of Belmore at a cost of over £26,000. They included '2 Very Superb Grecian Couches, double french stuffed … the entire executed in a very Superior Style' (now in

left: **One of the 'Very Superb Grecian Couches' designed by John and Nathaniel Preston for Castle Coole.**
opposite: **The Carlton House desk at Kingston Lacy takes its name from the Prince Regent's London house.**

The finest collections were given separate picture galleries

the Drawing Room) and, most magnificent of all, the mahogany state bed, which came complete with complex swagged and tasselled hangings of scarlet silk, secured with gilt anthemions. The bed is said to have been ordered in anticipation of a visit by George IV, but in the event he never came.

In 1808–16 Lewis Wyatt completed the main block of Tatton Park and supervised its decoration, which was – typically for the age and the architect – eclectic in style. The Entrance Hall is severe Greek Revival. The Music Room is furnished in the Louis XIV style with Boulle Revival pieces, mostly supplied by Gillows of Lancaster. The Drawing Room is Rococo Revival, although the settees here are much more massive than their Rococo models. They are also carved on the backs, as they were designed to stand in the middle of the room and be seen in the round. The pier-tables, which are supported on gigantic silvered swans, bear comparison with those designed by Sir Jeffry Wyatville for Windsor. The best of the Old Master paintings collected by Wyatt's patron, Wilbraham Egerton, are concentrated in this room. Thanks to the disruption caused by the French Revolution, continental Old Masters of the highest quality crossed the Channel for the first time in the Regency period. The finest collections were given separate picture galleries, like that at Attingham Park in Shropshire, which was designed in 1805 by the Prince Regent's favourite architect, John Nash.

The Tatton Library is plainer and more masculine in style than the Drawing Room but was meant to be used as a communal living room in a way that Humphry Repton suggested was an innovation of the Regency era. It was typical of Wyatt that he should have preserved T.F. Pritchard's original Rococo plasterwork of the 1760s in the Dining Room. At Lyme Park in Cheshire Wyatt worked in a seventeenth-century style that was sensitive to this old house, so that at this distance of time it is often difficult to tell his work from that which inspired it.

The style was revived in the 1930s by a group of cultured devotees, who collected Regency furniture and in 1937 founded the Georgian Group to campaign for the appreciation and preservation of Georgian architecture. They included Ralph Dutton, who in the late 1930s commissioned the architect-aristocrat Gerry Wellesley to remodel his library at Hinton Ampner in Hampshire in the Regency style.

opposite: The Picture Gallery at Attingham Park, designed by John Nash in 1805.

Regency 139

Egyptian Revival

The most ubiquitous Egyptian motif found in British houses is the obelisk – a tapering, square-section column, originally of granite. It symbolised the sun for the ancient Egyptians, who placed them in pairs in front of their temples. Obelisks have been imported to Europe since Roman times, and they were revived as a decorative motif during the Renaissance. They first started appearing in Britain in the Elizabethan period as modest finials, on chimneypieces and topping garden walls, as at Montacute in Somerset. Full-size obelisks made useful vertical accents in eighteenth-century landscape gardens, for instance at Stowe and Claremont, where they were surrounded by water.

Increasingly during the eighteenth century antiquarians such as Thomas Hope travelled to Egypt to see the spectacular remains of ancient Egypt for themselves. In 1799, two years after his visit, Hope started to create a museum for the antiquities he had amassed on his travels. His house in Duchess Street, London, contained an Egyptian Room, for which he also commissioned a new suite of two settees and four armchairs, part of which is now at Buscot Park in Oxfordshire. The shape of the chairs was classical, the wood – mahogany – came from the Caribbean, and the colours – black and gold – were firmly Regency, but the decoration was carefully based on Egyptian models, as Hope explained:

The crouching priests supporting the elbows are copied from an Egyptian idol in the Vatican; the winged Isis placed in the rail is borrowed from an Egyptian mummy case in the Institute in Bologna; the Canopuses [funerary urns] are imitated from the one in the Capitol; and the other ornaments are taken from various monuments at Thebes, Tentyris [Dedyra], &c.

The house, which was opened to the public by admission ticket in 1804, provoked mixed reactions. The architect George Dance commented: 'However much there might be amusement in seeing the House, ... it certainly excited no feelings of comfort as a dwelling.' Nevertheless, it proved influential, particularly as published in Hope's *Household Furniture and Interior Decoration* (1807). By 1805 Stowe House had an Egyptian Bedroom and an Egyptian Hall, the latter decorated with sphinxes, hieroglyphs and a sarcophagus-shaped heating stove. The same year Thomas Chippendale the Younger supplied a mahogany writing desk, library table and suite of eight chairs for the Library at Stourhead, in which Richard Colt Hoare, an antiquarian traveller like Hope, pursued his studies. In this case, the style was modestly applied in the form of little Egyptian heads, which were combined with classical philosophers. By 1807 the craze was at its height, as the poet Robert Southey noted: 'Everything now must be Egyptian: the ladies wear crocodile ornaments, and you sit upon a sphinx in a room hung round with mummies, and the long black lean-armed long-nosed hieroglyphical men, who are enough to make the children afraid to go to bed.'

Lord Byron nicknamed his old college friend William John Bankes 'the Nubian Discoverer' for his pioneering expeditions up the Nile in 1815 and 1818. Bankes recorded the elaborate mural paintings inside the temple at Abu Simbel and the remains of the temple of Isis at Philae. After several mishaps he managed to transport one of the pink granite obelisks from Philae to his home at Kingston Lacy in Dorset, where it was set up in the centre of the South Lawn, together with the sarcophagus of Amenomope. These Egyptian discoveries inspired Bankes to acquire modern designs in the same style, such as the Paris porcelain lampstand of *c.*1805 in the Saloon.

Fascination with ancient Egypt continued into the Victorian period, reaching its climax with Owen Jones's Egyptian Court at the Crystal Palace in 1854. It was reflected in John Marshall's neo-Egyptian Temple Mills in Leeds, where even the flax-spinning machines were decorated with Egyptian ornament, because the Egyptians had been the first to make linen from flax. (Marshall's fortune enabled his descendants to become country gentlemen and buy up large tracts of the Lake District, which are now in the care of the National Trust.) It also appears in James and Maria Bateman's Egypt garden at Biddulph Grange, with its topiary pyramid and statue of the Ape of Thoth, the Egyptian god of gardening.

The craze briefly revived in the 1920s, following Howard Carter's excavation of the tomb of Tutankhamen, which inspired cinemas, dance halls and even the 'Tutankhamen' stair carpet at Mr Straw's House in Worksop.

'Everything now must be Egyptian'

above: **The Paris porcelain lampstand of *c.*1805 at Kingston Lacy reflects W.J. Bankes's fascination with Egyptian antiquities.**
opposite: **The Egyptian carpet at Mr Straw's House was inspired by the excavation of Tutankhamen's tomb.**

Rococo Revival

The Rococo style flourished anew in the 1820s and 1830s and influenced the fluid, voluptuous rhythms of much mid-Victorian upholstered furniture, despite the disapproval of critics such as Walter Crane, who thought it 'afflicted with curvature of the spine'.

Paradoxically, the French Revolution had helped to engineer the Rococo Revival. Essentially Neo-classical in temperament, the revolutionaries associated the Rococo with everything that was worst about the old regime, believing it to be dissolute and fundamentally unserious. Guillotining French aristocrats brought their possessions onto the market – not just Rococo furniture and paintings, but entire suites of carved panelling *(boiseries)* in the same style from their Paris *hôtels*. These were bought by British aristocrats, such as the wife of the 5th Duke of Rutland, who incorporated them into her redecoration of Belvoir Castle in Rutland. Baron Ferdinand de Rothschild did the same at Waddesdon in the 1870s.

In the early nineteenth century the designer Benjamin Dean Wyatt promoted the 'Old French Style' (as it was somewhat vaguely called) to his elite patrons, who included the Duke of Wellington at Apsley House and the 2nd Duke of Sutherland at Stafford House. Many of the furnishings of these palatial London houses were Rococo in mood, but little distinction was made between the Louis XIV and XV styles. The paintings that hung on these walls were often similarly modern re-creations of a lost eighteenth-century world by artists such as William Mulready and C.R. Leslie, who furnished scenes from the novels of Goldsmith and Sterne with real Rococo furniture.

Leslie was one of the many artists who were invited to Petworth by the 3rd Earl of Egremont and drew inspiration from its interiors. The panelling in Petworth's White and Gold Room was once thought to be an original example of 1750s Rococo in the French style. It now turns out to have been made in 1828 for the

'Everything is in the now revived taste of Louis the Fourteenth; decorated with tasteless excrescences, excess of gilding'

Prince Pückler-Muskau, *c.*1824

3rd Earl by the carver Jonathan Ritson, who was perhaps drawing on engravings made a hundred years earlier by the French Rococo designer Nicolas Pineau. This is all the more odd in that the 3rd Earl was a devotee of the classically minded Emperor Napoleon. The panelling makes an instructive comparison with the genuinely eighteenth-century Rococo mirrors by Whittle & Norman that hang in this room.

Rococo survived the severity of both Neo-classicism and the Modern Movement. Its spirit was kept alive in the twentieth century by Rex Whistler (1905–44), who was particularly inventive in designing Rococo-style cartouches, in both his wall-paintings and his book illustrations.

opposite: **Rex Whistler's illustrations for Swift's *Gulliver's Travels* (1930) include Rococo cartouches.**

right: **The White and Gold Room at Petworth combines Rococo Revival panelling with genuine Rococo mirror frames.**

144 Historical Styles and Designers

The Norman style proved more suitable for prisons and churches than country houses

Norman Revival

This style is easier to identify than it is to find. It can most readily be recognised by its round-headed windows and 'dog-tooth' zigzag decoration. But according to its principal historian, Tim Mowl, the Norman Revival 'never really happened', and it is certainly true that, during its 200-year history, it was never widely popular.

Not surprisingly, the style was most often adopted for remodelling castles that had survived from the era of William the Conqueror. So William Mills adopted it when refacing the south front of the White Tower in the Tower of London in 1637–8, and Hugh May chose Norman for the Upper Ward of Windsor Castle in 1675–84 (later replaced by Jeffry Wyatville's pasteboard Gothick for the Prince Regent).

In the early eighteenth century Vanbrugh tried to create a new kind of castle architecture out the Baroque style (see p.84). The belvedere he built for the Duke of Newcastle at Claremont in 1715 dominates the surrounding landscape like a great Norman keep and came with battlements and round-headed windows that recalled that world. Robert Adam's early 'castle style' was influenced by Norman architecture, but the effect he wanted to create was essentially picturesque. He proposed a Norman castle for the grounds of Osterley Park complete with machicolations (projecting parapets) and a Windsor-like round tower. This was meant as a romantic folly and was never built; indeed, it is unlikely that Adam ever got round to considering what the interiors should look like.

The most complete surviving example of the Norman Revival is the vast Penrhyn Castle in Gwynedd, which was built by Thomas Hopper for the slate magnate G.H. Dawkins Pennant in 1822–37. The obvious style to choose for a castle would have been the late thirteenth-century Gothic of Edward I's border fortresses, but Dawkins Pennant may have wanted to hint at an even more ancient lineage and outdo the neo-Norman Gwrych Castle just along the coast, which had been finished less than ten years before. Penrhyn boasts a gigantic Norman keep and accurate Norman detail taken from the illustrations in the antiquarian John Carter's *Ancient Architecture of England* (1795–1814). The climax comes in the Staircase Hall, which is decorated with superbly carved neo-Norman gargoyles, zigzags and columns celebrating the source of the family wealth. No examples of Norman furniture survive, but this did not stop Hopper from applying the style to fitted carpets, sofas, water closets and many other modern features unknown to the Normans.

Penrhyn did not encourage others to build homes in the Norman style, which proved more suitable for prisons and for churches. At Killerton in Devon Sir Thomas Dyke Acland commissioned a chapel inspired by the Norman style of St Mary's, Glastonbury. His architect, C.R. Cockerell, who usually worked in the classical style, argued: 'do not think of neutralizing, castrating & emasculating the copy of that noble building, & flattering yourself that you have what will be worthy of the original – either have an original work altogether or a correct reproduction – a good copy, but let us not have half measures.' Acland settled for a good copy but with a rose window based on that in the Norman church at Barfreston in Kent. Cockerell has equally strong views on the interior fittings, rejecting the idea of figurative stained glass by Thomas Willement, who had worked at Penrhyn: 'English eyes (even of gentlemen Protestants) are commonly … ignorant of the human form divine … permit me to recommend that the holy Evangelists be worthily drawn – or turn we to arabesque, safe in our ignorance & absence of pretension.' Instead, Dean Liddell (the father of Alice in Wonderland) provided an abstract design of lozenge patterns for the windows, and one of Sir Thomas's relations designed a neo-Norman altar table.

The ghost of the Norman style survived into the twentieth century in the round-arched vaulting of the lobbies that connect the various corridors of Edwin Lutyens's Castle Drogo in Devon, perhaps the last castle to be built in Britain.

opposite, above: **Grotesque heads on the Grand Staircase at Penrhyn Castle.**
opposite, below: **The Grand Hall at Penrhyn.**

Indian Style

The Indian item you are most likely to find in a British country house is a tiger skin rug, but, fortunately, there have been more creative responses to Indian culture. In August 1691 'Young Sir John' Brownlow of Belton in Lincolnshire commissioned a set of tapestry hangings from John Vanderbank, Chief Arras Worker of the Great Wardrobe, 'to be of Indian figures according to ye pattern of the Queens [Mary] wch are at Kensington [Palace]'. The designs seem to have been based in part on Moghul miniatures like those given to the Bodleian Library by Archbishop Laud in 1640. In the seventeenth and eighteenth centuries the term 'Indian' was used very broadly to embrace anything east of India. So the Belton tapestry includes a Chinoiserie pagoda and carriages.

For a brief period following Robert Clive's conquest of India in the 1750s the Subcontinent was a place where men of enterprise could make large fortunes rapidly. Clive himself returned to Britain in 1767 worth more than a quarter of million pounds, which he invested in rebuilding Claremont in Surrey. The exterior was conventional Palladian, but the Eating Room was meant to celebrate his achievements in India and was furnished with Indian ivory chairs and large paintings of the key events in his career. Clive committed suicide in 1774 before the house was completed, and it was his son who formed the Clive Museum of Indian art, which is now displayed at Powis Castle in showcases inspired by Sezincote in Gloucestershire, one of the few true Indian Revival country houses in Britain.

Visitors to the Great Exhibition in 1851 compared the standard of craftsmanship and the imaginative design of the Indian exhibits favourably with the British contributions. Sir Charles Trevelyan of Wallington introduced government-sponsored Schools of Art to the Subcontinent in a well-meaning attempt to encourage Indian craftsmen. Unfortunately, it had exactly the opposite result, as local artists abandoned their local traditions, and India was flooded with cheaper, mass-produced Western imports. Rudyard Kipling's father, John Lockwood Kipling, who was Principal of the Mayo School of Art in Lahore, tried to reverse this process. When he was commissioned to design an Indian-style billiard room for the Tudor Gothic Bagshot Park in Surrey in 1884, he chose a team of Punjabi wood-carvers, who created 241 honey-coloured panels carved with floral and animal motifs, every one different and not all Indian. The result was an impressively complete interior, but it had little to do with the Punjab, where such wood-carvings would have been restricted to the doors, and it had little influence in Britain. He did, however, pass on his fascination with India to his son, whose Sussex

above: **Rudyard Kipling's bookplate was designed by his father, who ran the Mayo School of Art in Lahore.**

home, Bateman's, contains statuettes of Hindu deities, a lacquer marriage chest and other mementoes of his years in India.

Lord Curzon served as Viceroy of India in 1898–1906, at the highpoint of the British Raj. He worked tirelessly to preserve the Taj Mahal and India's other historic monuments:

As a pilgrim at the shrine of beauty I have visited them, but as a priest in the temple of duty have I charged myself with their reverent custody and their studious repair.

He also sponsored an exhibition of the best Indian arts and crafts to coincide with the Coronation Durbar in 1903, and he turned to Indian craftsmen for his wife's famous 'peacock dress', which was made from metal thread and Indian jewels on cloth of gold that would sparkle in the electric light of the Durbar ball. However, when he came to build new government offices in Calcutta, he modelled them on his family seat, the Palladian Kedleston Hall in Derbyshire, rather than choosing an indigenous style.

above: **An ivory-veneered settee and chair from Lord Curzon's Indian Museum at Kedleston.**
above left: **Detail from *The Tiger Hunt,* a French early nineteenth-century scenic wallpaper at Attingham Park.**

148 Historical Styles and Designers

above: **A Victorian *un*conversation-piece. Robert Scott Tait's view of Thomas and Jane Carlyle in the Sitting Room at 24 Cheyne Row.**
opposite: **A Staffordshire watch-stand of Shakespeare at Smallhythe Place in Kent.**

Victorian

The designers of the Victorian era (1837–1901) worked in almost every style described in this book. Queen Victoria's own residences reflected this confusion: Gothick Windsor Castle, Regency Buckingham Palace, Italianate Osborne, Scottish Baronial Balmoral and Neo-classical Claremont.

Some, like A.W.N. Pugin (see p.154), deplored the fact: 'The architecture of our times is not the expression of existing opinions and circumstances, but a confused jumble of styles and symbols borrowed from all nations and periods.' In Thomas Hardy's novel *A Laodicean* (1881) the hero, George Somerset, abandons architecture for literature in disgust, as the author himself had done:

When quite a lad, in the days of the French-Gothic mania which immediately succeeded to the great English-pointed revival under Britton, Pugin, Rickman, Scott and other mediaevalists, he had crept away from the fashion to admire what was good in Palladian and Renaissance. As soon as Jacobean, Queen Anne, and kindred accretions of decayed styles began to be popular, he purchased such old-school works as Revett and Stuart, Chambers, and the like, and worked diligently at the Five Orders; till quite bewildered on the question of style, he concluded that all styles were extinct, and with them all architecture as a living art.

Hardy himself comments, 'Somerset was not old enough at the time to know that, in practice, art had at all times been as full of shifts and compromises as every other mundane thing,' and he ends the novel with Somerset building himself a new house which is to be 'eclectic in style'.

Thomas Carlyle took an equal pleasure in swimming against the tide. He described the sitting room of his home in Cheyne Row as 'unfashionable in the highest degree, but in the highest degree comfortable and serviceable', but, as recorded by Robert Scott Tait in 1857–8, it reflects many aspects of the mid-Victorian middle-class interior. In the first place, the emphasis on comfort is very Victorian. The solid Regency-style mahogany chairs and the carpet were a family inheritance, but the Delft tiles in the fireplace and the floral wallpaper that hid the panelling had been added recently by the Carlyles. The prints cut out and pasted to the corner bracket bear witness to 'decalcomania', which swept the country in the 1860s. Above all, there is a sense that one is prying into a private world. As the French historian Hippolyte Taine noted, the dream of every Victorian man was for a home that would be 'his own little universe, closed to the world'. For Carlyle, his sound-proofed writing room upstairs certainly became this.

Tait took over a year to paint his interior with the aid of photography – one of the key Victorian inventions, which was pioneered by Henry Fox Talbot of Lacock Abbey in the 1830s. Photography did not yet convey colour, but from the 1840s it gives an unprecedented insight into how the Victorians decorated their houses. The overwhelming impression is one of *clutter*: not just a proliferation of objects, made possible by industrialisation and the consumer revolution that had begun in the eighteenth century, and kept clean by an army of servants, but a delight in pattern of all kind.

The overwhelming impression is one of *clutter*

To the design reformers of the mid-Victorian period, who inspired the Arts and Crafts movement (see p.166) with its credo of simplicity, all this abundance was anathema. Walter Crane dissected mid-Victorian domestic taste:

Big looking glasses, and machine made lace curtains, and where the furniture is afflicted with curvature of the spine, and dreary lumps of bronze and ormolu repose on marble slabs at every opportunity, where monstrosities of every kind are encouraged under glass shades, where every kind of design debauchery is indulged upon carpets, curtains, chintzes and wallpapers, and where the antimacassar is made to cover a multitude of sins.

Perhaps not surprisingly, this kind of interior is today preserved almost exclusively in photographs, and even where the fixed decoration has survived, the clutter has gone.

As soon as Carlyle died in 1881, his house was turned into a shrine to his memory. Commemorating great men was a very Victorian notion, which inspired the foundation of the National Portrait Gallery in 1856 and hundreds of public statues. Memorials were also incorporated into interior decoration, most commonly in the form of Staffordshire figures of the famous and the notorious that increasingly adorned Victorian mantelpieces. Great Northumbrians are depicted in roundel portraits in the Central Hall at Wallington, which is, in many other respects as well, a very Victorian space. In the first case, it had been reclaimed for private, domestic use by adding a glass roof to a central courtyard in 1853. Below the roundels were depicted important episodes in the history of the county, and wildflowers were painted on the piers between with Ruskinian precision; indeed, John Ruskin himself contributed one of the panels. In contrast, Thomas Woolner's statue of a mother and child symbolises the Victorian ideal vision of civilisation.

left: **These native poppies in the Central Hall at Wallington were painted with Ruskinian precision by Pauline, Lady Trevelyan.**
opposite: **The Drawing Room at Calke Abbey has been little altered since 1856.**

Victorian 151

Gothic Revival

The Gothic Revival took on a new form in the 1790s as a reaction to the dominance of Neo-classicism. It gradually abandoned the Gothick phase of the style (see p.104), becoming more serious and archaeologically correct. From the 1830s it was again the accepted style for churches and many other kinds of public building.

One man who helped to bring about this change was John Carter (1748–1817). He came from a family of marble carvers, who had supplied Palladian chimneypieces to numerous country houses. His father, Benjamin Carter, who had carved chimneypieces for Stourhead, introduced him to Westminster Abbey, 'the mortal repository of English glory', and John at once fell in love with medieval art. He disliked the term Gothic, preferring simply 'Pointed' (from its most obvious characteristic, the pointed arch) or 'English'. The campaign for Gothic took on an even more nationalistic flavour after the French Revolution: Carter refused to accept that English Gothic might owe anything to France, and he dismissed classicism because it was 'the invention of foreigners'. He became an architectural draughtsman for the Society of Antiquaries, recording the great English Gothic cathedrals, and also a polemical journalist, denouncing in forthright terms anyone who might threaten them. His greatest wrath was reserved for 'the Destroyer', James Wyatt, and his radical 'restoration' of ancient buildings such as Lichfield Cathedral (1787–93): 'All is *improvement* … everything is so smart, with *whitewashing*, *painting* and *glazing*. Ladies and gentlemen can now attend without fear of taking cold, or the dread of seeing anything to make them think about dying.'

In this respect, he heralded the conservation movement founded by William Morris (see p.164) that lives on in the work of the National Trust. In dismissing the sham Gothick of Wyatt and Nash ('this "cement" influenza') and advocating a new Gothic vernacular, which would be applied structurally, not as a surface decoration, he also anticipated A.W.N. Pugin (see p.154) and his Reformed Gothic successors. But like many conservationists, he was suspicious of change – 'Does innovation threaten? Forbid it, Taste! Forbid it, History' – and he built little himself. Typically modest is his extension to the Gothic Cottage at Stourhead of 1806. Carter's appreciation of Gothic remained more romantic than scholarly, and it was left to the next generation to unravel the historical development of the style and to apply the discoveries to new architecture.

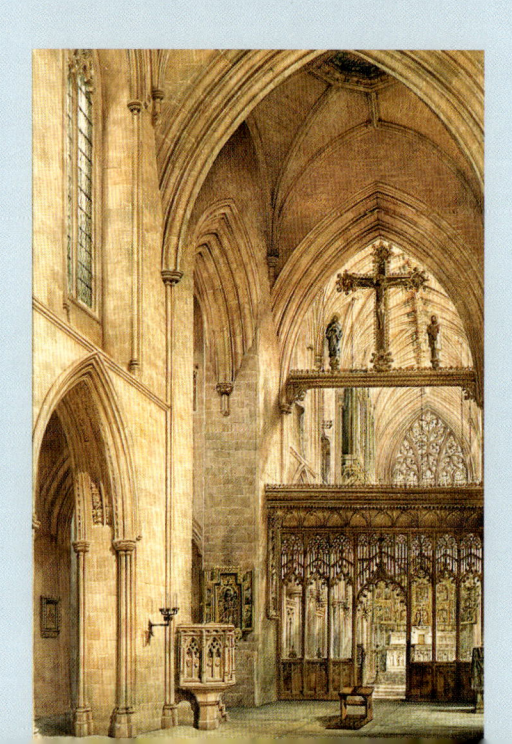

From the 1830s Pugin and his followers championed Gothic as the only proper style for Britain – not just for churches but for every kind of secular building and its fittings. So at Oxburgh Hall in Norfolk we find Gothic arches and tracery used to decorate items, such as sunblinds and wallpaper, that were unknown to the Middle Ages. The acceptance of Gothic as the national style was finally acknowledged in 1836, when the competition rules for the new Houses of Parliament stipulated that it must be built in the 'Gothic or Elizabethan' styles.

In the hands of Pugin's successors, such as William Burges (see p.156), William

Butterfield and G.E. Street, the Reformed Gothic style (as it became known) developed a new muscularity, influenced by the massive forms of thirteenth-century Early English Gothic. This is particularly evident in the Reformed Gothic furniture of the 1860s, which was bulky and architectural in form – perhaps not surprisingly, because most of the early examples were designed by architects. It followed Pugin's tenet of 'truth to construction' and was rarely mass-produced. It was also often richly coloured and densely decorated with medieval subjects. However, such pieces were usually heavy and uncomfortable to use and never found a wide market. Indeed, Reformed Gothic as a whole remained an exclusive taste.

From the 1870s young architects and designers increasingly developed a more refined and complex version of Gothic, drawing on the early fourteenth-century Decorated style. A fine example is the estate church built at Clumber Park in Nottinghamshire by G.F. Bodley and Thomas Garner in 1886–9 for the devoutly Anglo-Catholic 7th Duke of Newcastle. Bodley ensured that Gothic lived on into the twentieth century with his designs for Washington Cathedral, Washington, DC, although the style was by then restricted almost entirely to churches.

left: **A Gothic Revival blind at Oxburgh Hall.**
opposite: **A watercolour by H.W. Brewer of Bodley's design for Clumber chapel.**

above: **A teapoy designed by Pugin** c.1850 for Gawthorpe Hall.

A.W.N. Pugin
(1812–52)

Pugin was the central figure of the Gothic Revival and the most inventive, and ultimately the most influential, designer of the whole nineteenth century.

He was the precociously gifted only child of A.C. Pugin (c.1769–1832), a French *émigré* architectural draughtsman in the tradition of John Carter (see p.152). The elder Pugin was also a designer, who may have been responsible for a suite of Regency-style dining-chairs at Attingham Park in Shropshire. His son was designing furniture for the Prince Regent when he was fifteen years old.

A.W.N. Pugin adopted Gothic not just as a building style but as a way of life. He converted to Catholicism in 1835 and campaigned for Gothic with the moral fervour of the convert. Gothic was right because it was the expression of a society uncorrupted by the modern world. And Gothic was right because it was an honest and practical way of building. Pugin declared:

The two great rules for design are these: 1st, that there should be no features about a building which are not necessary for convenience, construction, or propriety; 2nd, that all ornament should consist of enrichment of the essential construction of the building.

Pugin found it hard to live up to these principles (which were later taken up by the Modern Movement and put to very

Gothic was the expression of a society uncorrupted by the modern world

different ends). Hence, perhaps, his continuing frustration with his masterpiece, the decoration of the Houses of Parliament, as this is, in planning at least, essentially a classical building.

Thanks to Pugin's fertile brain and immense energy, to a few devoted and wealthy patrons and, not least, to the mobility made possible by the railways, he was able to achieve a huge amount in a short life. At Chirk Castle in Clwyd he worked with J.G. Crace (see p.158) from 1845 to gothicise existing classical interiors. His best surviving room is the Cromwell Hall, for which he designed a traceried oak screen, heraldic panelling and stained glass, and a massive stone chimneypiece decorated with coats of arms. He also restored Jacobean furniture for the room and put up the brass gasolier, which happily adapted simplified Gothic forms to a modern device. (One suspects that Pugin would have had no difficulty coming up with elegant designs for TV aerials and satellite dishes.) But Pugin was a designer who knew that the devil was in the detail, and for that reason he disliked working at Chirk: 'I could make a church as easy as a grate. Such a job as Chirk is enough to drive any man mad. All little things are as difficult to get properly done as the greatest.'

At Gawthorpe Hall in Lancashire (a county that had remained faithful to Catholicism and where Pugin often worked) he collaborated in 1850–52 once again with the architect of the Houses of Parliament, Charles Barry, who was restoring the house in Elizabethan style. Pugin designed the decorative ironwork for the front door, incorporating an openwork KS monogram for the Kay-Shuttleworth family and a handle hung on weaver's shuttles. It was made by his favourite metalworkers, Hardman's of Birmingham. The Dining Room has wool and silk brocade curtains in the 'Gothic Tapestry' pattern Pugin designed in 1844, drawing on fifteenth-century Italian silk velvets used for altar frontals. The Drawing Room is furnished with an octagonal table similar to the one Pugin supplied for the Prince's Chamber in the House of Lords and with settees that have Pugin's distinctive square, chamfered legs. But most beautiful of all is the little teapoy, which is inlaid with a pattern of dog roses that demonstrates the very high standards of which the best Victorian craftsmen were capable. The Staircase Hall is floored with Minton's popular encaustic tiles, in patterns that Pugin had used at Westminster. The wallpaper in the Long Gallery has a pattern of stylised thistles, similar to the Drawing Room curtains, and an unusual flock paper border, simulating red Morocco leather. In most cases Pugin re-used earlier designs, but he also created a new wallpaper pattern specially for Gawthorpe. The diagonal fleur-de-lis and foliage motif is treated with a new freedom of design and colour that look forwards to the work of Morris & Co., but Pugin died in 1852 while still working on the Gawthorpe commission and before he was able to explore its possibilities any further.

right: **The Cromwell Hall is Pugin's best surviving interior at Chirk Castle.**
far right: **Pugin's brass gasolier in the Cromwell Hall at Chirk.**

> 'Ugly Burges who designs lovely things. Isn't he a duck'
>
> Lady Bute

William Burges
(1827–81)

Burges was perhaps the most inventive of the generation of 'Muscular Gothic' designers who came to prominence in the 1860s. He dreamed of jewel-like Gothic interiors and found the means and the craftsmen to make them a reality.

Billy Burges had a private income and never married, which meant that he could afford to take on fewer commissions than his contemporaries and devote more attention to each one. He relied on a small group of wealthy clients, above all, the super-rich 3rd Marquess of Bute, who could pay for the lavish detail and craftsmanship he demanded. 'There are no bargains in art,' was a favourite saying of his. He favoured the early to mid-thirteenth-century phase of Gothic, which was plainer than the 'middle pointed' style championed by Pugin and the ecclesiologists: 'I was brought up in the thirteenth-century belief and in that belief I intend to die.' He was also much influenced by French Gothic. His approach was essentially romantic and lacked the moralising fervour of Pugin. Humour was never far away.

In 1870 Burges completed the shell of a new house at Knightshayes in Devon for the Heathcoat Amory family. However, when in November 1873, he presented them with a grand album of his designs for the interior, they recoiled in horror and sacked him. Quite why the Heathcoat Amorys had turned to Burges in the first place remains something of a mystery. They were down-to-earth industrialists and country gentry with limited means and no wish to live in the Middle Ages – which is what Burges was proposing. Of Burges's planned interior, only the carved stone and woodwork were completed to his specification. The corbels in the Hall are carved with figures and stylised foliage in an Early English style reminiscent of Salisbury Cathedral. The corbels in the Billiard Room (the setting of many a Victorian misspent youth) take the form of animals representing the Seven Deadly Sins: a fat sow stands for Gluttony – a typically quirky Burges touch. The Trust has restored Burges's original Library ceiling with his characteristic gilt domelets, like flattened jelly-moulds, which were taken from Islamic architecture rather than Gothic. His most ambitious scheme was for the walls of the Drawing Room. He proposed to decorate this essentially feminine room with a mural on the theme of 'The Assault on the Castle of Love'. It was to take the form of a medieval castle: from the battlements, ladies were meant to look down on knights who have fallen in the assault, while in the frieze above there were to be 'figures showing the various conditions of life, offering their hearts to Cupid'. There was even supposed to be a gallery behind, so that the Heathcoat Amory women could themselves become part of the tableau. But this charming fantasy was all too much for the family.

Burges found more accommodating, and wealthier, clients in the Marquess and Marchioness of Ripon, who commissioned two ornate estate churches from him in Yorkshire. According to the Marchioness, that at Studley Royal, which was built in 1871–8, was 'designed at a moment's notice on the spot by Mr Burges, single-handed, the T-square and drawing board having been provided by Lady Ripon, so that the design might be made, as she said, by her architect and under her influence'. In fact, Burges took immense pains with the design and the decoration, which was entrusted to a skilled team, including his favourite sculptor, Thomas Nicholls, and the stained-glass designer, Fred Weekes. The interior is in Burges's preferred Early English style, with a double tracery screen borrowed from Ripon Cathedral. The decoration becomes increasingly lavish and colourful as you approach the chancel, which is enlivened with stained glass, wall-paintings and a host of carved angels from the Book of Revelation. For those who are used to the run-of-the-mill Victorian church interior, St Mary's, Studley Royal is a revelation indeed.

opposite: **The Middle Ages brought back to life. Burges's Winter Smoking Room at Cardiff Castle, as imagined by Axel Haig.**
right: **The Library ceiling at Knightshayes Court, which features Burges's characteristic 'jelly-mould' domelets.**

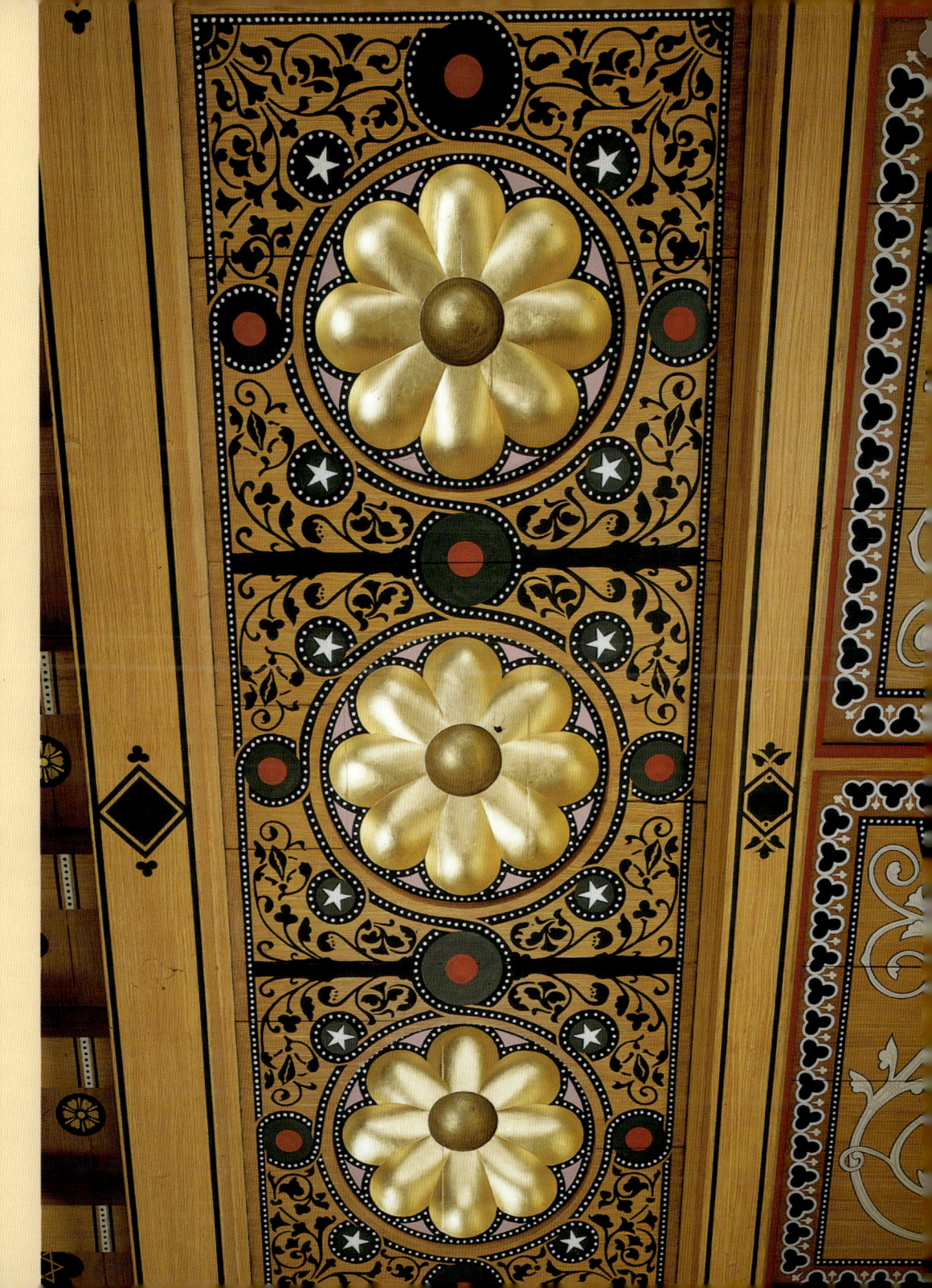

The pattern was carefully arranged to fit the room

right: **The Rococo Revival wallpaper in the Morning Room at Arlington Court was probably supplied by the Crace firm, like the Italianate pilasters and rose damask in the Boudoir (opposite).**

Crace Family

This influential firm of interior decorators was run by five generations of the same family between 1768 and 1899. It not only supplied furniture, *objets d'art*, textiles and wallpapers for fashionable interiors but also specialised in designing painted decoration for walls and ceilings in whichever style was in vogue.

The founder of the firm, Edward Crace (1725–99), decorated coaches in the Rococo style, but very little of his finished work has survived. His son, John (1754–1810), worked for Henry Holland on the Regency interiors of the Prince of Wales's Carlton House (see p.120). John's son, Frederick (1779–1859), decorated the Brighton Pavilion in the Chinoiserie style, again for the Prince of Wales.

The Crace firm reached its widest audience during the Victorian era, thanks to Frederick's son, John Gregory Crace (1809–89). After a tour of Paris to study French styles of interior decoration, in 1837 he opened a showroom in Wigmore Street, which was decorated in the 'early French Renaissance' style. J.G. Crace became a strong advocate of the 'Old French Style', a rather vague term, which embraced French forms of the Baroque, Rococo and Neo-classicism. One of his first customers was Sir John Chichester of Arlington Court in Devon, for which he probably supplied the green and cream Rococo Revival (see p.142) wallpaper in the Morning Room. The pattern was carefully arranged to fit the room with the help of additional floral motifs between the main repeats. Crace probably also designed the arabesque panels on the pilasters in the Boudoir, which match a motif on his invitation cards, and he may have provided the Louis XVI-style rose and gold silk damask wall-covering in the same room. J.G. Crace worked closely with A.W.N. Pugin (see p.154) to realise the latter's rich vision of a new Gothic style that would suit the modern world. Their most famous collaborations were on the interiors of the new Houses of Parliament from 1843 and on the Medieval Court at the 1851 Great Exhibition. In the 1840s Crace painted the heraldic ceiling for Pugin's recast Long Gallery at Chirk Castle.

John Dibblee Crace (1839–1919), who joined the firm in 1854, developed a much lighter version of his father's Gothic style, which he applied to the heraldic ceiling of the West Drawing Room at Oxburgh Hall in Norfolk. In 1874 he was called in at Knightshayes Court in Devon to provide a tamer and less expensive alternative to William Burges's fantasy medievalism (see p.156). Crace described his work here as 'in the earlier Gothic style of art' – an acknowledgement of his debt to Burges and to St Mark's Cathedral in Venice. He emphasised the beams of the Morning Room ceiling with chequer-work lines and stencilled the compartments sparely with quatrefoils and simple foliage patterns. His design for the Drawing Room fireplace, made from walnut, red Devon marble, alabaster and mirror glass and with shelves for displaying china, looks forward to the Art Nouveau style in its sweeping lines.

J.D. Crace's most elaborate surviving interior in a National Trust house is the Pompeian Room at Ickworth in Suffolk, which is illustrated on p.132. He made a particular speciality of the French Renaissance style, which he applied to the decorative surround of the Cliveden staircase ceiling for William Waldorf Astor, his most important client of the 1890s.

Renaissance Revival

Although the Gothic Revival has come to be seen as *the* Victorian style, classical remained the preferred style for town halls, banks, gentlemen's clubs and grand London residences, because the Victorian ruling class thought it projected the right message of security, prosperity and dignity.

But what kind of classicism to choose? The Victorians had tired of the plain perfection of the Greek Revival (see p.130) and were looking for a classical style with more gusto and richness of decorative detail. They found it in the *palazzi* (town houses) built by the great bankers and merchants of Renaissance Italy, with whom they instinctively identified.

The key figure in the Renaissance Revival was the architect Sir Charles Barry (1795–1860). Barry had been obliged to design the exterior of the Houses of Parliament in an Elizabethan style, but he planned the huge complex with Renaissance rationality, and he usually worked in an Italianate style. He applied the style not only to Pall Mall clubs but also to country houses, such as Trentham Hall in Staffordshire (now mostly demolished) and Cliveden in Buckinghamshire, both for the immensely wealthy 2nd Duke of Sutherland.

At Kingston Lacy in Dorset Barry was given less freedom by his client, William John Bankes. He had to work with an existing Restoration house, which Bankes wanted remodelled to look more Palladian, as Inigo Jones was then thought to have been the original architect. Bankes also had his own ideas about the interior, which was to include a Baroque staircase based on that in the Palazzo Ruspoli in Rome. Because of a sex scandal, Bankes had to flee abroad before the work was complete, but from his exile in Venice he was still able to supervise the decoration, much of which was done by Italian

left: **The boxwood doors in the Dining Room at Kingston Lacy were based on sculptures by Donatello.**
right: **The ceiling of the Golden Room came from the Renaissance Palazzo Contarini in Venice.**

craftsmen in a Renaissance Revival style. Grandest of all is the gilt and coffered ceiling in the Golden Room, which is said to have come from Scamozzi's Palazzo Contarini in Venice. For the Dining Room the Venetian carver Vincenzo Favenza made exquisite boxwood doors with reliefs based directly on Donatello's High Altar in the Santo at Padua – one of the masterpieces of early Renaissance sculpture.

Perhaps the greatest example of Renaissance Revival sculpture in any English country house is the spectacular marble chimneypiece in the Drawing Room, which was added to Cragside in Northumberland in 1883–4. The architect Richard Norman Shaw (1831–1912) had gradually extended the house in his suave version of the Old English style, but for this final showpiece he chose the French Renaissance style. His then chief assistant, W.R. Lethaby, came up with a confection of putti, swags, arabesques and strapwork. The quality of the marble-carving is of the highest order, as one might expect from the firm of Farmer & Brindley, which produced much of best Gothic Revival ornament in Sir George Gilbert Scott's churches.

Jacobethan

> Even the door-locks were given a vaguely Jacobethan form

'The mullioned and transomed Elizabethan [was the] never-to-be-surpassed style for the English country residence,' according to a character in one of Thomas Hardy's novels. Many Victorian owners of country houses agreed with this view, choosing a vague amalgam of the Elizabethan and Jacobean styles (nicknamed 'Jacobethan'), when they wanted to remodel the old or build anew.

Charlecote Park in Warwickshire had been built about 1551–8 for Sir Thomas Lucy, who had entertained Elizabeth I there for two nights in 1572. Even more famously, around 1583 Lucy is reputed to have caught the young William Shakespeare poaching his deer. George Hammond Lucy and his wife, Mary Elizabeth, were proud of these connections, and they decided to remove eighteenth-century alterations and to return Charlecote to its Elizabethan heyday after Lucy inherited the estate in 1823. Lucy was particularly fascinated by heraldry, commissioning a lavishly illuminated family tree, so it is not surprising that he should have sought help from the Heraldic Artist to George IV, Thomas Willement, who supervised the new decoration. Willement repaired the old heraldic glass in the Great Hall and added new coats of arms in the same style to record the succeeding generations. He also probably replaced the open timber ceiling of the Great Hall with beams and Tudor roses that may look convincingly

above: **A door-lock in the Oak Drawing Room at Powis Castle.**
opposite: **The Oak Drawing Room at Powis in 1905. Watercolour by H.C. Brewer.**

Elizabethan but were, in fact, made from painted plaster. Busts of Elizabeth I and Shakespeare stand beside Lucy ancestors.

In the Library hangs another portrait of the queen in a Jacobean-style frame carved in 1836 but inscribed 'Anno 1565', the year that the builder of the house was knighted by the queen's representative. The Library is Charlecote's most complete Jacobethan interior, with a heraldic carpet and much strapwork on the chair-covers and the bookcases, which were carved by J.M. Willcox, a leading member of the Warwick school of carvers, who was also responsible for the gigantic Charlecote buffet in the Dining Room. Willement designed the brown flock on gold leaf wallpaper, which has an interlace pattern that he told the Lucys was 'well suited to the style of your house'. The ivory-inlaid, ebony high-backed chairs were especially grand examples of a type then thought to be Elizabethan and, indeed, to have been presented by the queen to the Earl of Leicester in 1575.

Powis Castle in Powys has medieval walls, but its earliest surviving interior is Elizabethan – the Long Gallery decorated for Sir Edward Herbert in 1587–95 with a heraldic frieze, crudely illusionistic painted panelling and a compartmented plasterwork ceiling (see p.1). This provided the inspiration for G.F. Bodley's remodelling of much of the interior in 1902–4. Bodley was best known as a church architect working in a refined late Gothic style (see p.153), but he had impressed the 4th Earl of Powis with his sensitive restoration of another old mansion, Ham House in Surrey. To make the new Dining Room, he dismantled an old bedroom and pantry. His approach may seem fairly brutal to modern eyes, but the new work was carefully based on genuine Jacobean examples. So the two Dining Room fireplaces were copied from one in the Victoria & Albert Museum that the Earl particularly admired, which had been rescued from Bromley-by-Bow Palace and were carved with the Powis arms. The panelling adopted the pattern of the Jacobean woodwork in the dismantled pantry, and the ceiling was modelled on that in the Jacobean Reindeer Inn in Banbury (removed in 1912). Bodley went to the church furnishers Watts & Co. for fabrics, including the green cut-silk velvet in the Oak Drawing Room, which was made to his own bold 'Pear' pattern. Even the door-locks were given a vaguely Jacobethan form.

William Morris
(1834–96)

Morris was a designer and poet, a socialist and conservationist, the founder (in 1861) of the furnishing firm Morris, Marshall, Faulkner & Co. (later Morris & Co.) and, with John Ruskin, the inspiration of the Arts and Crafts movement (see p.166).

In his diary Morris described himself as a hater of 'all Classical art and literature' (although he made an exception for Homer). His passion was for Gothic architecture, not just in itself but as the expression of a more cohesive, pre-industrial society. He loved not only the great cathedrals but also humbler agricultural buildings, such as the early fourteenth-century Great Coxwell Barn in Berkshire, which he thought was 'the finest piece of architecture in England'. His attitude to furniture and the other products of Morris & Co. was similar. The firm made its name retailing 'necessary workaday furniture', such as the traditional rush-seated 'Sussex' chair, which Morris insisted should be 'simple to the last degree'. But it also sold much more elaborate and expensive 'state-furniture', which he described as 'the blossoms of the art of furniture'.

Morris was no good at drawing animals or people – he left that to his two closest friends and colleagues, the architect Philip Webb and the painter Edward Burne-Jones – but he was a master at pattern. He was inspired by the native plants that grew in his gardens at the Red House in Kent and Kelmscott Manor in Oxfordshire, which he drew with crispness and clarity: 'I must have unmistakable suggestions of gardens and fields, and strange trees, boughs and tendrils.' Morris had a particular genius for giving his plant designs a sense of fluid rhythm that seems entirely natural. As he explained in his 1881 lecture 'Some Hints at Pattern Designing', each branch 'grows visibly and necessarily from another' and has the potential for further, limitless growth.

Morris applied these principles with increasing subtlety to block-printed wallpaper and textiles and to woven fabrics. His patterns work especially well when they are used on curtains and other foldable materials. Luxuriant plant forms also appear in the backgrounds of the firm's tapestries ('the noblest of the weaving arts'), which from 1881 were made at its own factory at Merton Abbey in south London. But Morris saw tapestry as a more public art, which should have an accessible narrative, and so figures predominate, mostly designed by Burne-Jones, who also responsible for the majority of the firm's stained glass.

As a socialist, Morris wanted to bring good design to everyone, but his handmade products were not cheap, and inevitably he found himself 'ministering to the swinish luxury of the rich', as he put it. In fact, most of his customers came not from among the very rich but from the educated upper-middle classes – paint-makers, such as the Manders of Wightwick

Manor, or solicitors, such as the Beales of Standen – and his ideas were spread widely, in the first instance by his disciples, who dined at Gatti's restaurant after meetings of the Society for the Protection of Ancient Buildings: W.R. Lethaby, Sidney Barnsley, Ernest Gimson and Detmar Blow (who restored the Old Post Office at Tintagel on SPAB principles for the National Trust). The first substantial account of Morris's work was written by his friend Aymer Vallance, who went on to restore and extend a fifteenth-century timber-framed hall-house at Stoneacre in Kent – the kind of building that Morris cherished.

Morris wanted to bring good design to everyone

left: **Morris's 'Acanthus' wallpaper of 1875.** right: **A 'Sussex' settee against an embroidered wall hanging based on Burne-Jones's painting** *The Mill*, **at Wightwick Manor.**

Arts and Crafts

The Arts and Crafts movement represented a response to a sense of crisis in mid-Victorian society and design. Rapid industrialisation had brought social alienation and a mass of poorly designed products. The Victorian 'Battle of the Styles' between classical and Gothic and the revival of numerous other historical styles had created confusion and made some designers suspicious of the very idea of style.

The critic John Ruskin (1819–1900) championed the crisp but rough quality of handmade ornament, particularly as carved by medieval craftsmen. Many of the items displayed at the 1851 Great Exhibition had been made by hand, but they were more notable for their ingenuity than their beauty. Good design was also essential. This was to be achieved by a revival of traditional building materials and techniques and by breaking down the artificial barriers that had grown up between architect, artist and craftsmen and between the fine and decorative arts. The motto of the Art Workers Guild, which was founded in 1884 to bring these groups together, was 'the Unity of all the Aesthetic Arts'. (Women, however, were excluded.) For socialists such as William Morris (see p.164) and W.R. Lethaby, the Arts and Crafts movement embraced not only better designed products but also a whole way of life. As the designer C.R. Ashbee wrote, it 'means standards, whether of work or life ... and it means that these things must be taken together'.

The Arts and Crafts ideal of the good life and the total work of art was best achieved in the domestic interior and in houses like Standen in West Sussex, which was built by Philip Webb in 1892–4. Webb had been trained by G.E. Street in the Gothic tradition, but he refused to apply any stylistic label to his own work, which tried simply to provide a practical solution to contemporary needs using the best local materials. He took it as a great compliment if his buildings were described as commonplace. Despite this modestly functionalist approach, Webb's own personality as a designer could not help emerging. One sees it at Standen particularly in the fireplaces, each of which is different and offers plentiful surfaces on which to display pottery by William de Morgan and other Arts and Crafts ceramicists. Webb used colour and pattern sparingly but boldly. Typical are the red walls of the Entrance Hall and the sunflower motif on the *repoussé* metal wall-plates for the Drawing Room lights. Webb thought the spaces around an ornamental pattern were as important as the pattern itself and believed they should read as 'a mosaic pattern effective at a distance'.

left: **One of Philip Webb's deceptively simple chimneypieces at Standen. No two are the same.**
opposite: **A William de Morgan lustreware vase at Standen.**

'The Unity of all the Aesthetic Arts'

Motto of the Art Workers Guild, 1884

Ashbee, Gimson, Barnsley and many other Arts and Crafts designers settled in the Cotswolds in search of the simple life. One who followed them was Charles Paget Wade (1883–1956). Paget had been a solitary, day-dreaming child, whose only talents were for drawing and carpentry. He became an architect, working for the Arts and Crafts firm of Parker & Unwin, designers of Hampstead Garden Suburb, but he was most active as a book illustrator. A private income allowed him to move to Snowshill Manor in Gloucestershire, a typical Cotswold stone house, which he lovingly restored, preserving as much as possible of the original fabric. From an early age Wade had collected discarded examples of handmade English craftsmanship, which had once been commonplace but are now extremely rare. These he also restored and displayed with a sense of theatre throughout Snowshill, which represents the Arts and Crafts aesthetic taken to its furthest extreme.

opposite: **Herbert Horne's** *Angel with the Trumpet* **hanging at Stoneacre**.

above: **The Dining Room at The Grange, the Fulham home of Burne-Jones, who decorated the sideboard. Webb designed the table.**

Aesthetic

The Aesthetic Movement was the younger, more raffish brother of the Art and Crafts Movement. Rejecting William Morris's political engagement and devotion to nature, the late nineteenth-century aesthete believed that art was essentially useless, amoral and unnatural. Art and beauty were to be pursued for their own sake.

When it came to interior decoration, however, there were many links, perhaps best represented by one of the most influential aesthetes, the art critic Walter Pater (1838–94). In the 1870s his North Oxford drawing room was decorated with 'a Morris paper, spindle-legged tables and chairs; a sparing allowance of blue plates and pots ... framed embroidery of the most delicate design and colour ... engravings, if I remember right, from Botticelli or Luini, or Mantegna; a few mirrors, and a very few flowers, chosen and arranged with simple yet conscious art'. Oscar Wilde decorated his Oxford undergraduate rooms in just this fashion, adding huge bunches of white lilies. *Lilium auratum*, which had been introduced from Japan only in 1862, became the talisman of the aesthetes after Ruskin had blessed it as one of the most beautiful and useless things in the world. In praising Ellen Terry's performance as Henrietta Maria in 1879, Wilde compared her to 'some wan lily overdrenched with rain'. There could be no higher praise from an aesthete.

From 1868 to 1874 Terry had lived with the architect and designer E.W. Godwin, who was one of the central figures of the Aesthetic Movement. A protégé of William Burges (see p.156),

'Some wan lily overdrenched with rain'
Oscar Wilde on Ellen Terry

above: **The Aesthetic style spread rapidly. In this illustration from Mrs Loftie's** *The Dining Room* **(1878), the woman holds a Japanese fan and adopts the pose of Whistler's portrait of Mrs Leyland.**

opposite: **Ellen Terry in costume as Henrietta Maria.**

Godwin became fascinated with the furniture illustrated in Japanese woodcuts, which inspired his own designs for ebonised, spindly legged tables. The examples that he made for Ellen Terry are still to be seen at her country home, Smallhythe Place in Kent. Terry shared his passion for all things Japanese, dressing their two children in Japanese kimonos from an early age.

When Wilde wanted to redecorate his Chelsea home at 16 Tite Street in 1884–5 it was no surprise that he should have turned to Godwin to create 'the House Beautiful'. The front door was painted white, and shades of white predominated inside, contrasted with blue, green and gold. There were no Morris wallpapers. The library was decorated in Moorish style, with low divans and no chairs

172 Historical Styles and Designers

'One of the most beautiful and useless things in the world'

Ruskin on the lily

(Victorian clutter was to be banished). Running round the frieze was a stanza from Shelley's 'Spirit of Beauty'. The white-painted stairs were covered with golden-yellow matting. The second-floor drawing room had dark green walls, on which hung Whistler lithographs in white frames. On the pale green ceiling Whistler also painted two gold dragons. A statue of Narcissus (the classical personification of self-absorbed beauty and so the perfect symbol of the Aesthetic Movement) stood on the mantelpiece.

Whistler was also responsible for the most famous of all Aesthetic interiors, the Peacock Room. His client was the shipping magnate F.R. Leyland, who had invited Whistler to Speke Hall near Liverpool to paint his wife. Her full-length portrait from behind (now in the Frick Collection, New York) is one of the most beautiful images of the Aesthetic Movement. Leyland put up Morris wallpapers at Speke but was only renting the house so went no further. In his London home in Prince's Gate he could be altogether more ambitious.

There Whistler painted golden peacocks on a deep sea green background, with numerous shelves built into the walls to display Leyland's famous collection of blue-and-white porcelain. Unfortunately, Whistler got carried away by the scheme and by the beauty of Mrs Leyland, and was sacked.

Wilde and Whistler were both accomplished self-publicists, Wilde even lecturing on Botticelli to the coal-miners of West Virginia. Satires, including Gilbert and Sullivan's *Patience* (1881), only helped to spread the message. As a result, the ideas of the Aesthetic Movement were disseminated widely in a watered-down form. And this spare style did not need to be expensive. So by the end of the century, there were few middle-class homes without an 'artistic' touch – a peacock feather or a Japanese fan – on the mantelpiece.

left: **Nina Cust in her library at Chancellor's House, Hyde Park Gate.**

174　Historical Styles and Designers

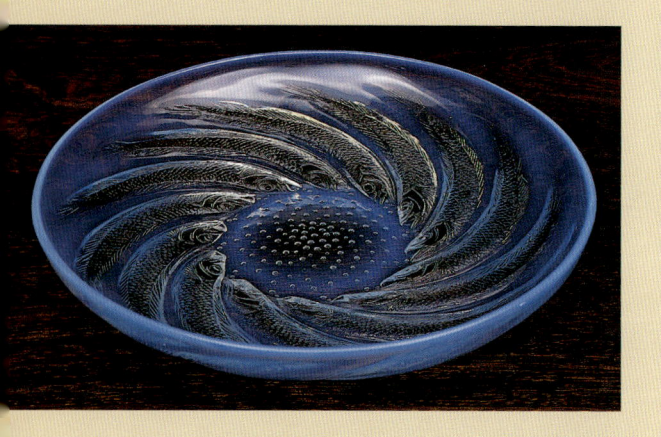

left: **An iridescent blue bowl designed by René Lalique, one of the creators of the French Art Nouveau style.**
right: **Aubrey Beardsley's design for a poster advertising the 1894 season at the Avenue Theatre, London:** 'Advertisement is an absolute necessity of modern life, and if it can be made beautiful as well as obvious, so much the better for the makers of soap and the public who are likely to wash.'

Art Nouveau

Art Nouveau simply means 'new art' in French. Despite the vagueness of the term, it is usually easy to recognise, by its sinuous lines and pleasure-loving mood, both derived from the Rococo. It came to prominence at the 1900 world fair in Paris and spread rapidly across Europe, most effectively through the medium of the exhibition poster, one of the key Art Nouveau devices. For a short while, Art Nouveau became a universal European style, as Neo-classicism had been 150 years before.

In England, however, the new style was greeted with considerable suspicion. Art Nouveau was essentially metropolitan and middle-class and so found even less favour with the owners of English country houses. The most talented British designer in the style, Charles Rennie Mackintosh, received little work or appreciation in England. In 1901 he drew the ruins of Lindisfarne Castle in Northumberland, but when the new owner wanted to remodel the building as a holiday home the following year, he chose Edwin Lutyens as his architect and Arts and Crafts as the style.

Yet there are important links between Arts and Crafts and Art Nouveau, personified by the figure of Aymer Vallance, who was both a protégé of William Morris (see p.165) and a mentor of Aubrey Beardsley, the one major Art Nouveau artist that England produced. In January 1892 the nineteen-year-old Beardsley showed Vallance some of his pen-and-ink drawings. Their bold calligraphy and louche subject-matter came as 'nothing less than a revelation'. Vallance introduced Beardsley to artist friends, including William Morris, but Morris dismissed the young artist as a mere plagiarist of Burne-Jones.

Although Vallance became increasingly concerned by the decadent strain in Beardsley's work, he kept faith with him, producing the first catalogue of his drawings. In 1893 he also advised on the decoration of Beardsley's new home in Pimlico. Bright orange walls contrasted with black-painted furniture, woodwork and floors to create one of the few Art Nouveau interiors in London.

The following year Beardsley designed a poster to advertise a season of plays at the Avenue Theatre in London, which included the première of Bernard Shaw's *Arms and the Man*. The visibility of the poster and the ambiguity of the woman's pose – is she merely an actress behind a stage curtain or perhaps a prostitute soliciting for business from her window? – only increased Beardsley's notoriety. This Beardsley design came to rest at Shaw's defiantly untasteful home, Shaw's Corner in Hertfordshire, which contains one other Art Nouveau feature, the

It was through the medium of coloured glass that the Art Nouveau style was most widely accepted into the English home

stained-glass panel beside the front door. It was through the medium of coloured glass that the Art Nouveau style was most widely accepted into the English home, and it is still to be seen in the fanlight of many a suburban semi. Art Nouveau and electric lighting spread simultaneously, and electric light-fittings proved particularly well suited to the style. The American glass-maker Tiffany specialised in making coloured glass shades in the Art Nouveau style for electric lights, similar to those in the Drawing Room at Bateman's in East Sussex.

Edwardian

The bored-looking features of Edward VII stare out from hundreds of stiffly posed photographs of country-house parties, but during his brief reign (1901–10) there was a marked relaxation in upper-class codes of behaviour. Although he has a reputation as a philistine, more interested in shooting, eating and female company than in his surroundings, several members of his circle were avid collectors and decorators.

Mrs Ronnie Greville was typical of this world. The illegitimate daughter of a wealthy Edinburgh brewer, in 1906–9 she commissioned the firm of Mewès and Davis to transform Polesden Lacey from a plain Regency villa into a luxurious and comfortable mansion fit to entertain royalty. (The king duly visited in 1909.) Mewès and Davis had made their name building the Paris and London Ritz Hotels, and Polesden was given all the modern conveniences of a luxury hotel, with numerous extra bedrooms, capacious baths and marble-topped sinks, and – most important of all – a brilliant French chef. New money paid for old woodwork, such as the Entrance Hall reredos salvaged from Christopher Wren's City church of St Matthew's. A cast of Jacobean plasterwork filled the barrel ceiling of the Picture Corridor. Edwardian opulence reached its height in the Saloon, which was lined with early seventeenth-century gilt panelling from a south Italian *palazzo*. Plentiful quantities of Louis XV and XVI furniture and Chinese porcelain added to the somewhat overpowering atmosphere of luxury.

Edwardian interior decorators were capable of greater subtlety. One of the most interesting was Percy Macquoid (1852–1925), whose work was grounded in a thorough knowledge of English furniture, published in *The Age of Walnut* (1905) and *The Age of Mahogany* (1906). In 1906 the 9th Earl of Stamford asked him to advise on the redecoration of Dunham Massey in Cheshire, to which the family had recently returned after a long absence. A Victorian architect would probably have recast this ancient house in a uniform Jacobethan style. Macquoid's approach was altogether more sensitive and eclectic. He added a classical anthemion frieze to the Saloon, a room with a bow window and scagliola Ionic columns that had been created in 1822, but most of his efforts went into getting the colours and textures of the furnishings right. He painted the walls apple green and dyed the Donegal carpets moss green. Contrasting tones were provided by the pale yellow, silk damask curtains, the golden-yellow, eighteenth-century Gillows bookcases and the brown, cut-silk chair-covers, which were, like most of the fabrics in the house, supplied by Morant & Co, a firm specialising in historic interiors. Macquoid urged the Stamfords to make sure that nothing red was allowed into the room. He cheered up the rather daunting Great Hall by painting the walls yellow and adding more plasterwork in late seventeenth-century style. Historical good manners were less necessary in the Summer Parlour, which, as a result, is the most thoroughly Edwardian room in the house, with bright floral chintzes giving it a relaxed character typical of the era.

left: **Sargent's portraits capture the more unbuttoned mood of the age. Indeed, he had originally wanted Nancy Astor to pose with her young son clinging to her back.** opposite: **The Saloon overmantel at Polesden Lacey. 'It was a sumpshuous spot all done up in gold with plenty of looking glasses' (Daisy Ashford, *The Young Visiters*, 1919).**

> All the modern conveniences of a luxury hotel, with numerous extra bedrooms, capacious baths and marble-topped sinks

177

Art Deco

The style, which flourished in the 1920s and 1930s, was French in origin, taking its name from the Exposition Internationale des Arts Décoratifs et Industriels Modernes held in Paris in 1925. (Moderne was the name given to the later stages of the same phenomenon.) In reaction to the fluid forms of Art Nouveau, Art Deco favoured geometric shapes, derived in part from a somewhat simplistic understanding of Cubism. Increasingly during the 1930s it celebrated the modern and the machine age, with much use of metal, glass and strong colour, but it happily pillaged motifs, such as the ubiquitous sunrise, from earlier sources, such as Egyptian art (see p.140).

Americans loved the style. Even the conservative-minded Charles Henry Robinson, who wanted to live in ancient Ightham Mote in Kent, had his whisky tumblers engraved in Art Deco style. The style was adopted more hesitantly for new domestic building in Britain, where a cosier neo-Tudor (see p.162) was generally preferred for the suburban semi, the dominant building type of the period. When Rupert D'Oyly Carte commissioned a new holiday home at Coleton Fishacre in south Devon in 1923, he opted for a plain Arts and Crafts style for the exterior. Inside, however, there are many Art Deco touches: most obviously, the stepped outlines of the Drawing Room door-surround and overmantel mirror and of the Corridor ceiling lights. Dorothy D'Oyly Carte's bedroom was furnished with a bold floral fabric, designed in 1919 by the French artist Raoul Dufy, who had earlier worked for Paul Poiret, one of the key Art Deco figures in France (see p.6).

Art Deco interiors often incorporated murals, such as the bird's-eye view of the south Devon coast in the Library overmantel at Coleton Fishacre. The most spectacular Art Deco mural in a National Trust house is Leon Bakst's cycle of 'Sleeping Beauty' at Waddesdon Manor, which was commissioned by James de Rothschild in 1913, the year that Bakst burst on the London scene as the designer for the first Covent Garden season of Diaghilev's Ballets Russes. The costumes and architectural detail in the Rothschild panels may be medieval, but the lush colours are unmistakably Art Deco.

Art Deco became the favoured style for luxury hotels, cinemas and other places of entertainment. Unsurprising, therefore, that Rupert D'Oyly Carte should have chosen it for the interiors of Claridge's and the new Savoy Theatre in 1929–30. His designer, Basil Ionides, upholstered the theatre seats in startlingly vivid shades of red, orange and yellow, randomly arranged, and covered the walls in shimmering silver leaf. Ionides's brother-in-law was the 2nd Viscount Bearsted, who was remodelling Upton House in Warwickshire around the same time. For the most part the interiors are in a conservative Queen Anne style, but in the bathroom Bearsted opted, perhaps with Ionides's encouragement, for a more adventurous Art Deco treatment, with a vaulted, aluminium leaf ceiling and red columns.

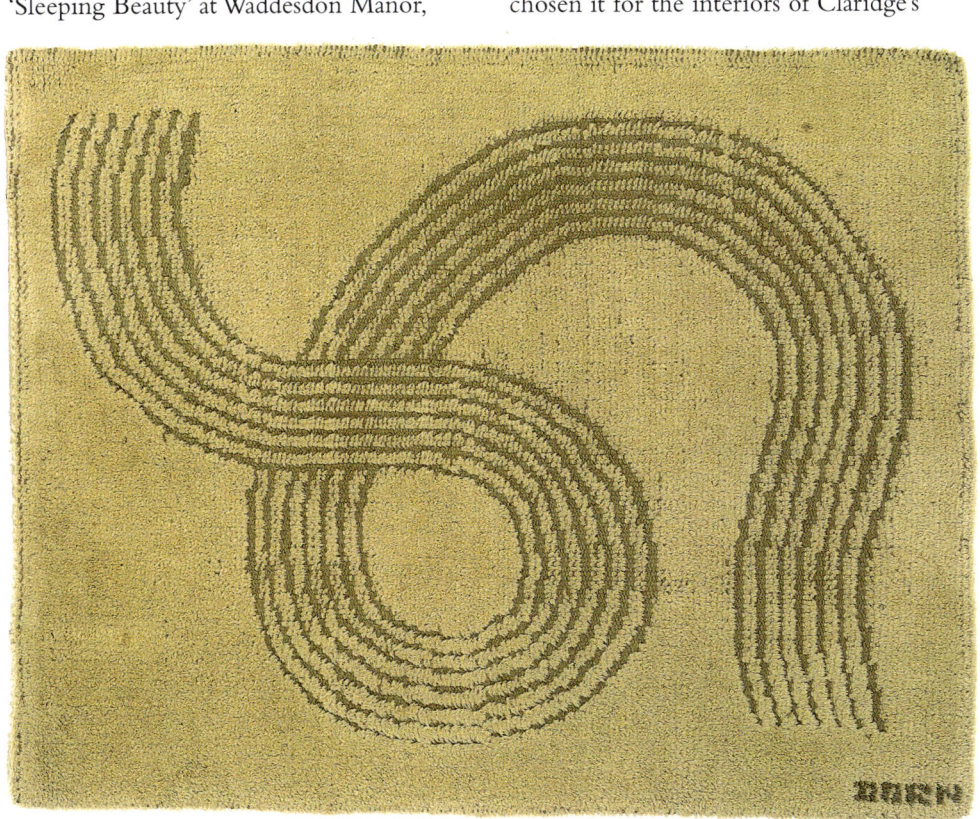

left: **Marion Dorn's carpet at Coleton Fishacre.**

opposite: **The aluminium leaf bathroom at Upton House.**
above: **One of Edward Bawden's bathroom tiles at Coleton Fishacre.**

Modern Movement

From the outside the Modern Movement house is easy to identify – and to caricature – as a white-painted, flat-roofed box that fails to keep out the rain. Like many new styles that originated abroad, the Modern Movement was accepted only grudgingly in Britain, and hardly at all by the conservative country-house building class. When the style was finally applied to high-rise flats in the 1960s, it was blamed for a social disaster that is still with us. So it is perhaps not surprising that the National Trust owns only two Modern Movement houses, both acquired recently.

Like the Huguenot silversmiths in the 1690s, many Modernist designers in the 1930s came to Britain from the Continent to flee persecution. Among them was the young Hungarian architect Ernö Goldfinger (1902–87), who had been trained in Paris in the studio of Auguste Perret, one of the pioneers in the artistic use of reinforced concrete. Goldfinger found it hard to get work at first and so became his own client, building 2 Willow Road for his family as part of a terrace of three houses overlooking Hampstead Heath in 1937–9. To win over the doubtful planning authorities, Goldfinger emphasised that it was to be largely faced in traditional brick and that its form and proportions owed much to the Regency terrace, which he greatly admired: 'Only the Esquimeaux and the Zulus build anything but rectangular houses.' However, the skeleton beneath the skin was more radical: large concrete floor slabs supported on concrete pillars, which dispensed with the need for fixed internal walls and so made a more flexible, open-plan existence possible.

The naked shuttering of the pillars recalls the fluting of a classical column, but they have no capitals or plinths, and the traditional language of ornament is completely absent. Animation is provided by light, which floods in through the floor-to-ceiling windows; by pure geometrical forms, like the circular skylights above the bathroom and the top landing; by colour (such as the brilliant red walls of the spiral staircase); and by the contents. The first photographs of the house show barely furnished rooms, which gradually filled during Goldfinger's long life, as rooms tend to do. Goldfinger himself designed much of the furniture, which made great use of bent plywood, tubular steel and sliding 'tambour' screens, behind which the clutter was meant to be hidden. Like Robert Adam before him, he paid attention to such small details as the door handles, which were shaped to fit the hand but also to look elegant. Modernist ideals even influenced his headed writing paper, for which he chose the sans serif Futura typeface, created by Paul Renner in Berlin in 1927. Beautiful and legible typography remains one of the most enduring achievements of the Modern Movement.

A white-painted, flat-roofed box that fails to keep out the rain

In 1937 the 24-year-old Patrick Gwynne managed to persuade his parents to demolish their Victorian home near Esher in Surrey and let him build them a new house in the Modern style. Their faith was rewarded. As its name suggests, the Homewood stands among trees, which the wide expanses of glass bring into the interior. As at Willow Road, light-filled, flexible spaces were the aim. Great effort also went into getting the surfaces right. There is little traditional decoration, apart from the folding screen painted with a pattern of bamboo, which divides the sitting room from the dining room. The old family portraits are framed with minimal metal fillets.

181

opposite: **Ernö Goldfinger's 1977 perspective of the Studio and Living Room at 2 Willow Road. Concrete floor slabs allowed for a more flexible, open-plan interior.**
right: **Like most Modern Movement architects, Goldfinger also designed furniture, using mass-production processes to make new forms.**

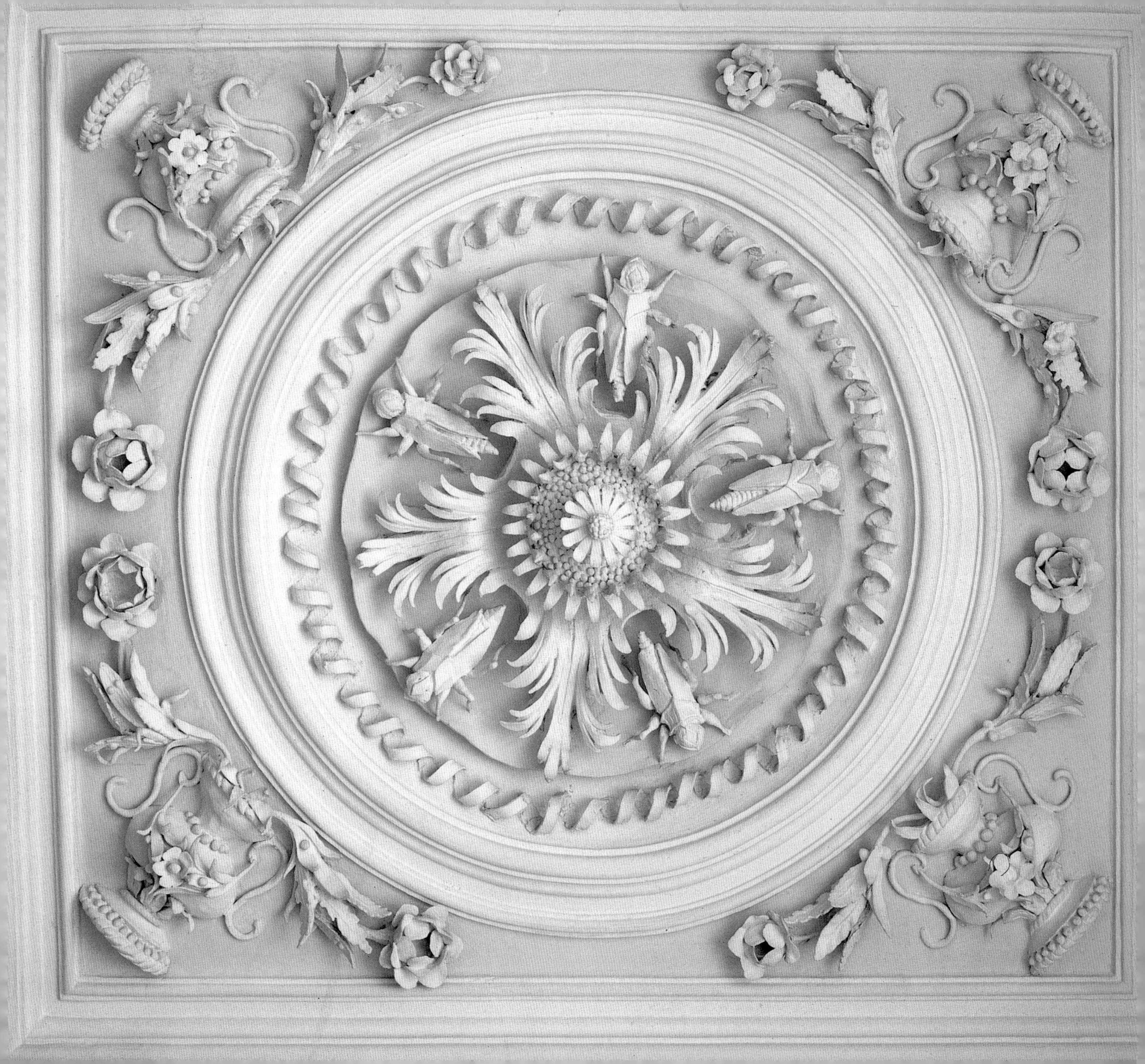

John Fowler
(1906–77)

John Fowler is not nearly as well known as Adam, Pugin, Morris and the other designers featured in this book, and Fowler himself preferred to be described as a decorator rather than a designer. Yet in his role as consultant on decoration to the National Trust from 1956 until his death in 1977, Fowler had as much influence on the way historic country houses look today as any of these great names.

A decorator rather than a designer

John Fowler started out in the 1930s designing smart flats in Chelsea and Mayfair, in 1938 joining Sybil Colefax to form the interior-decorating firm of Colefax & Fowler, which still flourishes. As he explained that year, his ideal room ought to be 'well behaved but free from too many rules … to be comfortable, stimulating, even provocative, and finally to be nameless of period'. Fowler's favourite style was that which flourished at the French court around the third quarter of the eighteenth century – the era of Louis XVI (see p.128) and Marie-Antoinette – but he had the confidence to mix bold colours and patterns from any age to create 'a "fantasie" expressing the personality of its owner'.

After the Second World War Fowler concentrated increasingly on restoring historic houses where the decoration had become tired. He respected the patina of age and was often content simply to wash down and retouch old paintwork rather than repaint. Fowler loved the apparently untouched Regency decoration of Uppark in Sussex – 'as delicate and fragrant as the bloom on a grape'. But he was often faced with large, no longer inhabited rooms that had lost the indigenous furniture, fabrics and clutter that made them seem 'lived-in'. His response was to use colour to animate the space and the surviving plasterwork and wood-carving, which were often the most interesting surviving aspects of the room. So the Great Hall at Sudbury in Derbyshire was painted a strong Italian pink, and the famous ceiling plasterwork of the Long Gallery was picked out in subtle shades of off-white. Vibrant yellows dramatise Sudbury's huge Staircase Hall and Claydon's equally large North Hall.

Fowler pioneered the analysis of paint scrapes to identify old decorative schemes, and he acquired a formidable knowledge of historic interiors, which was distilled in his book, *English Decoration in the 18th Century*. But he preferred to rely on his decorator's eye rather than on archival research in making the final choice of paint colour or fabric. Later, perhaps less self-confident, generations have criticised Fowler for not abiding by the historical evidence in restoring a room. As a result, some Trust houses have since been 'defowlerised'. Fowler himself would have been the first to acknowledge that tastes change in the presentation of historic houses, as in everything else: 'Each generation will restore country houses in different ways just as they will decorate them in different ways.' Yet he would have argued that restoration must remain a matter of aesthetic judgement as well as scholarship: 'It is to be hoped that the element of decoration will continue to influence approaches to restoration. Then at least there will be a striving after a sense of life and not just slavish renewal of the misguided taste of the day before yesterday.'

opposite: **The Long Gallery ceiling plasterwork at Sudbury was repainted by Fowler.**

above: **Fowler devised the yellow and white scheme for the Staircase Hall at Sudbury Hall.**

Bibliography

General

John Fleming and Hugh Honour, *The Penguin Dictionary of the Decorative Arts*, Penguin, Harmondsworth, 1977

Susan Lambert ed., *Pattern and Design: Designs for the Decorative Arts 1480–1980*, Victoria & Albert Museum, London, 1983

Peter Thornton, *Authentic Decor: The Domestic Interior 1620–1920*, Weidenfeld & Nicolson, London, 1984

Geoffrey Beard, *Craftsmen and Interior Decoration in England 1660–1820*, Bloomsbury Books, London, 1986

Simon Jervis, *The Penguin Dictionary of Design and Designers*, Penguin, Harmondsworth, 1986

Philippa Lewis and Gillian Darley, *Dictionary of Ornament*, Cameron Books/David & Charles, Newton Abbot, 1986

J. Mordaunt Crook, *The Dilemma of Style*, John Murray, London, 1987

Michael Snodin and Maurice Howard, *Ornament: A Social History since 1450*, Yale University Press, London, 1996

Geoffrey Beard, *Upholsterers & Interior Furnishing in England 1530–1840*, Yale University Press, London, 1997

Peter Thornton, *Form & Decoration: Innovation in the Decorative Arts 1470–1870*, Weidenfeld & Nicolson, London, 1998

John Morley, *Furniture: The Western Tradition: History, Style, Design*, Thames & Hudson, London, 1999

Introduction: Seeing Patterns

E.H. Gombrich, 'Styles of Art and Styles of Life', *1990 Reynolds Lecture*, Royal Academy, London, 1991

1: Questions of Style

What is Style?

John Ruskin, *Fors Clavigera*, 1871–84, in *Collected Works*, iv, p.39

E.H. Gombrich, 'Style', *International Encyclopedia of the Social Sciences*, Macmillan, New York, 1968, x, pp.352–61

Not What it Seems

Ian C. Bristow, *Architectural Colour in British Interiors, 1615–1840* and *Interior House Painting Colours and Technology, 1615–1840*, Yale University Press, London, 1996

Anthony Wells-Cole, *Art and Decoration in Elizabethan and Jacobean England*, Yale University Press, London, 1997

Mixing Styles

Lady Llanover ed., *Autobiography and correspondence of Mary Granville, Mrs Delany*, London, 1861–2, iv, p.20–21

Style & Status

Katie Scott, *The Rococo Interior*, Yale University Press, London, 1995, pp.101–17

David Cannadine, *Class in Britain*, Yale University Press, London, 1998

Nicholas Cooper, *Houses of the Gentry, 1480–1680*, Yale University Press, London, 1999, pp.13–18 ('The Sanctions for Display')

Thomas Woodcock and John Martin Robinson, *Heraldry in National Trust Houses*, National Trust, London, 2000

Consuming Style: London

Neil McKendrick, John Brewer and J.H. Plumb, *The Birth of a Consumer Society: The Commercialization of Eighteenth-Century England*, Hutchinson, London, 1983

John Brewer and Roy Porter ed., *Consumption and the World of Goods*, Routledge, London, 1993

Hilary Young ed., *The Genius of Wedgwood*, Victoria & Albert Museum, London, 1995

Consuming Style: The Grand Tour

Jeremy Black, *The British Abroad: The Grand Tour in the Eighteenth Century*, Sandpiper Books, Stroud, 1992

Andrew Wilton and Ilaria Bignamini ed., *Grand Tour: The Lure of Italy in the Eighteenth Century*, Tate Gallery, London, 1996

John Ingamells, *A Dictionary of British and Irish Travellers in Italy 1701–1800*, Yale University Press, London, 1997

Transmitting Style: The Sixteenth Century

Wells-Cole, 1997

David Bostwick, 'The Jacobean Plasterwork at Gawthorpe and its Sources', *Apollo*, May 1994, pp.24–8

Transmitting Style: The Seventeenth and Eighteenth Centuries

A.E. Richardson, *Decorative Details of the Eighteenth Century by William and James Pain*, Tiranti, London, 1946

Gervase Jackson-Stops, 'French Ideas for English Houses: The Influence of Pattern-Books, 1660–1700', *Country Life*, 29 January 1970, pp.261–66

Eileen Harris, *British Architectural Books and Writers, 1556–1785*, Cambridge University Press, 1990, esp. pp.32–37 [books of designs and pattern-books]

Elizabeth White, *Pictorial Dictionary of British 18th Century Furniture Designs: The Printed Sources*, Antique Collectors Club, Woodbridge, 1990

Antony Griffiths, *The Print in Stuart Britain, 1603–1689*, British Museum, 1998, pp.266 [ornament prints]

Transmitting Style: The Nineteenth Century

H.J.P. Arnold, *William Henry Fox Talbot*, London, 1977

Gail Buckland, *Fox Talbot and the Invention of Photography*, Boston, 1980

John Beckett, *The Rise and Fall of the Grenvilles*, Manchester University Press, 1994, pp.241–7 [for Stowe sale]

Oliver Garnett, 'Sold Christie's. Bought Agnew: The Art Collection of Lord Armstrong at Cragside', *Apollo*, April 1993, pp.253–8

Clare Norman, 'Rebecca Orpen's Country House Tour: A Portfolio of Watercolours at Baddesley Clinton', *Apollo*, April 1997, pp.28–32

Revivalism

David Adshead, 'The 2nd Earl of Buckinghamshire's work at Blickling: "Gothic it was, and more Gothic it will be"', unpublished paper given at *Historicism in the early 18th Century*, National Trust study day, October 2000

The Period Room

Roy Strong, *When did you last see your father?*, Thames & Hudson, London, 1978

Clive Wainwright, *The Romantic Interior*, Yale University Press, London, 1989

John Harris, 'A cautionary tale of two "period" rooms', *Apollo*, July 1995, pp.56–7

Amelia Peck and James Parker, *Period Rooms in the Metropolitan Museum of Art*, New York, 1996

Bruno Pons, *The James A. de Rothschild Bequest at Waddesdon Manor: Architecture and Panelling*, London, 1996

The Victoria & Albert Museum sponsored a conference on 'The Museum and the Period Room' in 1997, but the proceedings have not yet been published.

Country House Style

John Cornforth, *The Inspiration of the Past*, Viking, 1985

2: Components of Style

The Classical Orders

John Summerson, *The Classical Language of Architecture*, revised edition, Thames & Hudson, 1980

John Onians, *Bearers of Meaning: The Classical Orders in Antiquity, the Middle Ages and the Renaissance*, Princeton, 1988

Ingrid Rowland transl., Vitruvius, *Ten Books on Architecture*, Cambridge University Press, 1999

Doric

Giles Worsley, 'The baseless Roman Doric column in mid-eighteenth-century English architecture: a study in neo-classicism', *Burlington Magazine*, May 1986, pp.331–9

Arabesque

Peter Ward-Jackson, *Some Main Streams and Tributaries in European Ornament from 1500 to 1750*, Victoria & Albert Museum Bulletin, 1967, pp.5–14

E. Kühnel, transl. by R. Ettinghausen, *The Arabesque: Meaning and Transformation of an Ornament*, Graz, 1976

Snodin and Howard, 1996, pp.192ff

Grotesque

Frances K. Barasch, *The Grotesque: A Study in Meanings*, Mouton, The Hague, 1971

Peter Ward-Jackson, *Some Main Streams and Tributaries in European Ornament from 1500 to 1750*, Victoria & Albert Museum Bulletin, 1967, pp.5–14

Snodin and Howard, 1996, pp.36–41

3: Historical Styles & Designers

Renaissance

Mark Girouard, 'The Haynes Grange Room', reprinted in *Town and Country*, Yale University Press, 1992, pp.171–86

Karen Hearn ed., *Dynasties*, Tate Gallery, 1995, cat. no.14

Simon Thurley, *Tudor Royal Palaces*, Yale University Press, 1993

Tudor

Maurice Howard, *The Early Tudor Country House*, George Philip, London, 1987

Hearn, 1995, cat. no.76

Elizabethan

Roy Strong, *The Elizabethan Image: Painting in England, 1540–1620*, Tate Gallery, 1970

Mark Girouard, *Robert Smythson and the Elizabethan Country House*, Yale University Press, 1983

The Treasure Houses of Britain, National Gallery of Art, Washington/Yale, 1985, cat. no.32, pp.108–9

Caroline

The Age of Charles I, Tate Gallery, London, 1972

The Treasure Houses of Britain, Yale University Press, London, 1985, cat. nos.57–60

Alastair Laing and Nino Strachey, 'The Duke and Duchess of Lauderdale's Pictures at Ham House', *Apollo*, May 1994, pp.3–9

Baroque

Rupert Gunnis, *A Dictionary of British Sculptors*, Odhams Press, London, 1953, pp.72–4 [Bushnell]

Edward Croft-Murray, *Decorative Painting in England 1537–1837*, 1962, 2 vols.

A.M. Giusti, *Pietre Dure: Hardstone in Furniture and Decoration*, London, 1992

Restoration

R.T. Gunther ed., *The Architecture of Sir Roger Pratt*, Oxford University Press, 1928, pp.75–6

E.S. de Beer ed., *The Diary of John Evelyn*, Oxford University Press, 1959

Geoffrey Beard, 'Edward Goudge: The Beste Master in England', *National Trust Studies*, 1979, pp.21–7

Liza Picard, *Restoration London*, Weidenfeld & Nicolson, 1997, pp.36–53

David Esterley, *Grinling Gibbons and the Art of Carving*, Victoria & Albert Museum, 1998

Louis XIV

Gervase Jackson-Stops, 'English Baroque Ironwork – I: The Sources of Tijou's Designs; II: The Influence of Tijou', *Country Life*, 28 January 1971, pp.182–4, 4 February 1971, pp.262–6

Boulle

Hugh Honour, *Cabinet Makers and Furniture Designers*, Weidenfeld & Nicolson, 1969, pp.48–55

Theodore Dell, *The Frick Collection*, vi: *Furniture and Gilt Bronzes*, Princeton University Press, 1992

Peter Hughes, *The Wallace Collection: Catalogue of Furniture*, London, 1996, 3 vols

William and Mary

The Orange and the Rose: Holland and Britain in the Age of Observation, 1600–1750, Victoria & Albert Museum, London, 1964

Michael Archer, 'Delft at Dyrham', *The National Trust Year Book 1975–6*

Courts and Colonies: The William and Mary Style in Holland, England and America, Cooper-Hewitt Museum, New York, 1988

Gervase Jackson-Stops, 'Courtiers and Craftsmen: The William and Mary Style', *Country Life*, 13 October 1988, pp.200–9

Daniel Marot (c.1663–1752)

Peter Thornton, *Seventeenth-century Interior Decoration in England, France and Holland*, Yale University Press, London, 1978

Gervase Jackson-Stops, 'Daniel Marot and the 1st Duke of Montagu', *Nederlands Kunsthistorisch Jaarboek*, 1981, pp.244–62

Georgian

John Steegman, *The Rule of Taste from George I to George IV*, Macmillan, London, 1936

John Gloag, *Georgian Grace: A Social History of Design from 1660 to 1830*, A. & C. Black, London, 1956

M. Dorothy George, *Hogarth to Cruikshank: Social Change in Graphic Satire*, Allen Lane, London, 1967

Margaret Willes, *Scenes from Georgian Life*, National Trust, London, 2001

James Gillray: The Art of Caricature, Tate Britain, London, 2001

Palladianism

Peter Ward-Jackson, 'The Furniture of the Palladian Age', *English Furniture Designs of the 18th Century*, HMSO, 1958, pp.7–8

Desmond Guinness, *The Palladian Style in England, Ireland and America*, Thames & Hudson, London, 1974

Robert Tavernor, *Palladio and Palladianism*, Thames & Hudson, 1991

Stephen Parissien, *Palladian Style*, Phaidon, London, 1994

Giles Worsley, *Classical Architecture in Britain*, Yale Press, London, 1995, pp.197–212

William Kent (1685–1748)

Christopher Gilbert, 'James Moore the Younger and William Kent at Sherborne House', *Burlington Magazine*, March 1969, pp.148–9

Michael I. Wilson, *William Kent*, Routledge & Kegan Paul, London, 1984

Ingamells, 1997, pp.569–71

Gothick

Lilian Dickins and Mary Stanton ed., *An Eighteenth-century Correspondence*, John Murray, London, 1910, pp.301–10 [Miller at Lacock]

Gothick, 1720–1840, Art Gallery & Museums, Brighton, 1975

A Gothick Symposium, Georgian Group, 1983

Clive Wainwright, *The Romantic Interior*, Yale University Press, London, 1989

Cathal Moore and Christine Sitwell, 'Spiridione Roma at The Vyne: Reconstructing the work of a "very idle" painter', *Apollo*, April 1998, pp.25–9

Amin Jaffer, *Furniture from British India and Ceylon*, Victoria & Albert Museum, 2001, pp.130–35

Rococo

Helena Hayward, *Thomas Johnson and English Rococo*, Alec Tiranti, London, 1964

Mark Girouard, 'Coffee at Slaughter's: English Art and the Rococo', *Town and Country*, Yale University Press, London, 1992

Rococo, Victoria & Albert Museum, London, 1984

Charles Hind ed., *The Rococo in England*, Georgian Group, 1986

Jeremy Musson, 'The Shell House, Hatfield Forest, Essex', *Country Life*, 27 August 1998, pp.48–50

Timothy Mowl and Brian Earnshaw, *An Insular Rococo*, Reaktion Books, London, 1999

Louis XV Style

Bruno Pons, *Grands Décors Français 1650–1800*, Editions Faton, Paris, 1995

Scott, 1995

Chinoiserie

Hugh Honour, *Chinoiserie*, John Murray, London, 1961

John Harris, *Sir William Chambers*, Pennsylvania State Univeristy Press/Zwemmer, 1970

Patrick Conner, *Oriental Architecture in the West*, Thames & Hudson, London, 1979

Thomas Chippendale (1718–79)

Christopher Gilbert, *The Life and Work of Thomas Chippendale*, Studio Vista, London, 1978

Neo-classicism

The Age of Neo-classicism, Arts Council, 1972

John Martin Robinson, 'R.J. Wyatt's "Flora and Zephyr" at Nostell Priory, *National Trust Year Book, 1977–78*, pp.30–4

Damie Stillman, *English Neo-classical Architecture*, Zwemmer, London, 1988, esp. i, pp.111–36, 273–336

Robert Adam (1728–92)

John Fleming, *Robert Adam and his Circle in Rome & Edinburgh*, John Murray, London, 1962

Maurice Tomlin, *Catalogue of Adam Period Furniture*, Victoria & Albert Museum, London, 1972

Damie Stillman, *The Decorative Art of Robert Adam*, Academy Editions, London, 1973

Leslie Harris, *Robert Adam and Kedleston*, National Trust, London, 1987

David King, *The Complete Works of Robert and James Adam*, Butterworth, 1991

Louis XVI

Svend Ericksen, *Early Neo-classicism in France*, Faber, London, 1974

Geoffrey de Bellaigue, *Sèvres Porcelain in the Collection of Her Majesty the Queen: The Louis XVI Service*, Cambridge, 1986

Greek Revivalism

David Watkin, *Thomas Hope and the Neo-classical Idea*, John Murray, London, 1968, pp.61–92

J. Mordaunt Crook, *The Greek Revival*, John Murray, London, 1972

David Watkin, *Athenian Stuart*, George Allen & Unwin, London, 1982

S. Bury and M. Snodin, 'The Shield of Achilles by John Flaxman, RA', *Art at Auction*, 1983–4

Kerry Bristol, 'The Society of Dilettanti, James 'Athenian' Stuart and the Anson Family', *Apollo*, July 2000, pp.46–54

Pompeian

Pompeii as Source and Inspiration: Reflections in Eighteenth- and Nineteenth-century Art, University of Michigan, Museum of Art, [1977]

John Wilton-Ely, 'Pompeian and Etruscan Tastes in the Neo-classical Country-house Interior', in G. Jackson-Stops ed., *The Fashioning and Functioning of the British Country House*, National Gallery of Art, Washington, 1989, pp.51–74

Alastair Laing, *In Trust for the Nation*, National Gallery, 1994, cat. no. 31

Nino Strachey, 'The Pompeian Room at Ickworth', *Apollo*, April 1997, pp.8–12

Regency

Gervase Jackson-Stops, 'A Temple made tasteful: A Regency upholsterer at Castle Coole', *Country Life*, 10 April 1986, pp.918–20

Carlton House: The Past Glories of George IV's Palace, Queen's Gallery, Buckingham Palace, 1991

Stephen Parissien, *Regency Style*, Phaidon, London, 1992

John Morley, *Regency Design*, Zwemmer, London, 1993

Charles O'Brien, 'Ralph Dutton and Ronald Fleming at Hinton Ampner House', *Apollo*, April 1997, pp.43–7

Egyptian Revival

James Steven Curl, *The Egyptian Revival*, Allen & Unwin, London, 1982

Patrick Conner ed., *The Inspiration of Egypt*, Brighton Museum, 1983

Egyptomania, National Gallery of Canada, 1994

Rococo Revival

Carol Duncan, *The Pursuit of Pleasure: The Rococo Revival in French Romantic Art*, Garland, New York, 1976

Simon Jervis, 'The Rococo Revival', *High Victorian Design*, Boydell Press, 1983, pp.37–40

Gervase Jackson-Stops, 'Some sources for the paintings of C.R. Leslie', *The Magazine Antiques*, January 1989, pp.311–21

Gervase Jackson-Stops, 'Living with the Louis', *Country Life*, 1 October 1992, pp.72–3, fig.10

Norman Revival

David Watkin, *The Life and Work of C.R. Cockerell, RA*, Zwemmer, 1974, pp.178–81

Timothy Mowl, 'The Norman Revival', *Influences in Victorian Art and Architecture*, Society of Antiquaries Occasional Paper VII, 1985, pp.41–8

Gervase Jackson-Stops, *English Arcadia*, National Trust, 1992, no.75, pp.102–4

Jonathan Marsden, '"Far from elegant, yet exceedingly curious": Neo-Norman furnishings at Penrhyn Castle', *Apollo*, April 1993, pp.263–70

Indian Style

Edith A. Standen, 'English Tapestries "after the Indian Manner"', *Metropolitan Museum Journal*, xv, 1981, pp.119–42

Raymond Head, 'Bagshot Park and Indian Crafts', *Influences in Victorian Art and Architecture*, Society of Antiquaries, Occasional Paper VII, 1985, pp.139–49

Raymond Head, *The Indian Style*, University of Chicago Press, 1986

The Raj: India and the British 1600–1947, National Portrait Gallery, 1990

James Raven, *Judging New Wealth*, Clarendon Press, Oxford, 1992, pp.221–33

Amin Jaffer and Deborah Swallow, 'Curzon's ivory chairs at Kedleston', *Apollo*, April 1998, pp.35–39

Victorian

Susan Lasdun, *Victorians at Home*, Weidenfeld & Nicolson, London, 1981

Asa Briggs, *Victorian Things*, Batsford, London, 1988, especially pp.213–59

Charles Newton, *Victorian Designs for the Home*, Victoria & Albert Museum, London, 1999

John Tosh, *A Man's Place: Masculinity and the Middle-Class Home in Victorian England*, Yale University Press, London, 1999

Alastair Laing, *National Art Collections Fund Review*, 1999, p.70 [Robert Scott Tait's *A Chelsea Interior*]

Gothic Revival

Kenneth Clark, *The Gothic Revival*, John Murray, London, 1962

Simon Jervis, 'The Reformed Gothic Style', *High Victorian Design*, London, 1983, pp.99–121

Megan Aldrich, *The Gothic Revival*, Phaidon, London, 1994

J. Mordaunt Crook, 'John Carter and the Mind of the Gothic Revival', *Society of Antiquaries Occasional Paper*, no.17, 1995

Chris Brooks, *The Gothic Revival*, Phaidon, London, 1999

A.W.N. Pugin (1812–52)

Phoebe Stanton, *Pugin*, Thames & Hudson, London, 1971

Alexandra Wedgwood, *Catalogue of the Architectural Drawings in the Victoria & Albert Museum: A.W.N. Pugin and the Pugin Family*, Victoria & Albert Museum, London, 1985

Paul Atterbury and Clive Wainwright ed., *Pugin: A Gothic Passion*, Victoria & Albert Museum/Yale University Press London, 1994

Paul Atterbury ed., *A.W.N. Pugin: Master of Gothic Revival*, Bard Graduate Center/Yale University Press, London, 1995

William Burges (1827–81)

J. Mordaunt Crook, *William Burges and the High Victorian Dream*, John Murray, London, 1981

J. Mordaunt Crook ed., *The Strange Genius of William Burges, 'Art-Architect', 1827–1881*, National Museum of Wales, Cardiff, 1981

The Crace Family

John Cornforth, 'Arlington Court, Devon', *Country Life*, 30 April 1981, pp.1178ff

Megan Aldrich ed., *The Craces: Royal Decorators, 1768–1899*, John Murray, London, 1990

Renaissance Revival

Simon Jervis, 'The Renaissance Revival', *High Victorian Design*, Boydell, 1983, pp.123–43

Jacobethan

John Hardy and Clive Wainwright, 'Elizabethan-Revival Charlecote Revived', *National Trust Year Book 1976–7*, pp.12–19

Clive Wainwright, 'Charlecote Park', *Country Life*, 21, 28 February 1985, pp.446–50, 506–10

Wainwright, 1989, pp.208–40

Michael Hall, 'Powis Castle, Powys', *Country Life*, 21 October 1993, pp.80–3

William Morris (1834–96)

Aymer Vallance, *The Art of William Morris*, G. Bell & Sons, London, 1897

Fiona MacCarthy, *William Morris: A Life for our Time*, Faber, London, 1994

Linda Parry ed., *William Morris*, Victoria & Albert Museum, London, 1996

Arts & Crafts

Gillian Naylor, *The Arts and Crafts Movement*, Trefoil, London, 1971

Peter Davey, *Arts and Crafts Architecture*, Architectural Press, London 1980

Linda Parry, *Textiles of the Arts and Crafts Movement*, Thames & Hudson, London, 1988

Elizabeth Cumming and Wendy Kaplan, *The Arts and Crafts Movement*, Thames & Hudson, London, 1991

Art Nouveau

Matthew Sturgis, *Aubrey Beardsley: A Biography*, HarperCollins, 1998

Paul Greenhalgh ed., *Art Nouveau, 1890–1914*, Victoria & Albert Museum, 2000

Stephen Escritt, *Art Nouveau*, Phaidon, 2000 [both reviewed by Rosemary Hill, *Times Literary Supplement*, 5 May 2000]

Stephen Calloway and Susan Owens, 'A "lost" Beardsley drawing rediscovered', *Apollo*, April 2001, pp.49–54

Edwardian

Clive Aslett, *The Last Country Houses*, Yale University Press, London, 1982

Jane Beckett and Deborah Cherry ed., *The Edwardian Era*, Phaidon/Barbican Art Gallery, London, 1987

Jane Morrison, 'Macquoid at Dunham Massey', *Country Life*, 2 July 1987, pp.156–60

J. Mordaunt Crook, *The Rise of the Nouveaux Riches*, John Murray, London, 1999

Art Deco

Basil Ionides, *Colour and Interior Decoration*, Country Life, London, 1926

Arthur Oswald, 'Upton House', *Country Life*, 5, 12 September 1936, pp.248–53, 274–9

Martin Battersby, *The Decorative Thirties*, Studio Vista, London, 1971

Diana Souhami, *Bakst: The Rothschild Panels of the Sleeping Beauty*, Philip Wilson, London, 1992

Bevis Hillier and Stephen Escritt, *Art Deco Style*, Phaidon, London, 1997

Modern Movement

['The Homewood'], *Architectural Review*, September 1939, pp.103–16

['Willow Road'], *Architectural Review*, April 1940, pp.126–30

Neil Bingham, 'The Homewood, Surrey', *Country Life*, 22 July 1993, pp.84–7

'The Modern House Revisited', *Twentieth Century Architecture 2*, 1996

Neil Bingham, 'The Houses of Patrick Gwynne', *Post-War Houses, Twentieth Century Architecture*, iv, 2000, pp.29–44

John Fowler (1906–77)

Cornforth, 1985

John Fowler and John Cornforth, *English Decoration in the 18th Century*, Barrie & Jenkins, London, 1986

Tim Knox, 'John Fowler and the National Trust', unpublished paper given at *Inspired by the Past* conference, July 2001 [on John Fowler's approach to decoration and restoration in National Trust houses]

Index

acanthus pattern wallpaper 53, *165*
acanthus scroll ornament 52–3, *53*, 71
Acland, Sir Thomas Dyke, 10th Bt (1787–1871) 145
Adam, Robert (1728–92) 11, 15, 43, 44, 52, 54, 59, 66, 68, 84, 119, 120, 124, *126–127*, 127, 134, 145
    Works in Architecture 120, 124
Aesthetic Movement 170–1, 173
Anglesey Abbey, Cambs. *48*, *50*, 103, *103*, *105*, 109, 130
Anne, Queen (1665–1714) 97
Anson, Thomas (1695–1773) 130
anthemion 54–5, *55*
Antwerp 26–7
arabesque 57, *57*
architecture, classical orders 42–51
Ardress, Co. Armagh *40–41*
Arlington Court, Devon *158*, 159, *159*
Art Deco 17, *55*, 178–9
Art Nouveau *174*, 175
Art Workers Guild 166
Arts and Crafts 17, 164, 166, 169, 175
Ash, Graham Baron 38, *39*
Ashbee, Charles Robert (1863–1942) 166, 169
Astor, Nancy (1879–1964) *176*
Astor, William Waldorf (1848–1919) 159
Attingham Park, Shropshire 52, *120*, *122*, 123, 129, *129*, 138, *139*, 147, 154
auricular frames 82, *83*

Baddesley Clinton, Warks. 12, *13*
Bagshot Park, Surrey 146
Bakst, Léon (1866–1925) 179
Bankes, William John (1786–1855) 141, *141*, 160
Banqueting House, Whitehall 84
Barnsley, Sidney (1865–1926) 165, 169
Baroque style 52, 84–5
Barry, Sir Charles (1795–1860) 155, 160
Basildon Park, Berks. 37, *46*, 59
Bateman, James (d. 1897) and Maria (d. 1895) 15, 141
Batemans, East Sussex 147, 175
Bath Assembly Rooms 22, *98*, *98*
Batoni, Pompeo (1708–87) 24, *24*
Bawden, Edward (1903–89) 179
Beardsley, Aubrey (1872–98) *174*, 175
Bearsted, Walter (Samuel), 2nd Viscount (1882–1948) 179
Beckford, William (1760–1844) *14*, 104

Bedingfeld, Sir Henry (1511–83) 74, 136
Bedingfeld, Margaret (d. 1514) 74, *75*
Belton House, Lincs. 55, *66*, 71, *71*, 85, 86, 107, *121*, 146
Beningbrough Hall, North Yorks. *51*, 92, 95, *95*, 115
Bérain, Jean (1640–1711) 61, 94
bergère armchairs 110, *112*
Bernini, Gian Lorenzo (1598–1680) 84
Berrington Hall, Herefordshire 44, 47, *47*, 66, 68, 69, 123, *123*
Berwick, Thomas Henry (Noel-Hill), 8th Baron (1877–1947) 123
Berwick, Thomas Noel (Hill), 2nd Baron (1770–1832) 123
Bianchini Férier archive 6
    pattern-book *7*
Biddulph Grange, Staffs. 15, 116, 141
Blenheim Palace, Oxon. 97
Blickling Hall, Norfolk 32, 37, 65, *81*
Blondel, Jacques-François (1705–74) 19
Blow, Detmar (1867–1939) 165
Blum, Hans, *The Book of Five Columns* 47
Bodiam Castle, East Sussex 18
Bodley, George Frederick (1827–1907) 152, *153*, 163
Bonomi, Joseph (1739–1808) 133
Booth, George, 2nd Earl of Warrington (1675–1758) 97
Boucher, François (1703–70) 109, 110
Boulle, André-Charles (1642–1732) 52, 90–1, *90*, *91*, 92
Brighton Pavilion, East Sussex 115, 159
Bristol, Frederick (Hervey), 4th Earl of [Bishop of Derry] (1730–1803) 123, *133*
Bromley-by-Bow Palace 163
Brownlow, Sir John (1659–97) 146
bureau Mazarin 89, *91*
Burges, William (1827–81) 20, 152, 156–7, *156*, *157*
Burlington, Richard Boyle, 3rd Earl of (1694–1753) 100, 103
Burne-Jones, Sir Edward Coley (1833–98) 164, *165*, 169
Bushnell, John (*c.* 1630–1701) 85
Butterfield, William (1814–1900) 152–3

Calcutta government offices 147
Calke Abbey, Derbyshire *151*
Callimachus (*c.* 430–400 BC) 49
Campbell, Colen (1676–1729), *Vitruvius Britannicus* 28, 85
Canons Ashby, Northants. 47, *57*, 58, 68, 77, 78–9, 97, *97*
Canova, Antonio (1757–1822) *122*, 123
Cardiff Castle *156*
Carlin, Martin (*c.* 1730–85) 128, *129*
Carlton House, Pall Mall 13, 120, 129, 136, *136*, 159
Carlyle, Jane Baillie (née Welsh) (1801–66) *148*
Carlyle, Thomas (1795–1881) *148*, 149, 150
Caroline style 82

Carter, Benjamin (d. 1766) 152
Carter, John (1748–1817) 152
    Ancient Architecture of England 145
cartouches 58, *58*
Castle Coole, Co. Fermanagh 44, 136, *137*, 138
Castle Drogo, Devon 145
Castle Ward, Co. Down 15, *16*, 17, *17*, 68
Chambers, Sir William (1723–96) *42*, 116
Chancellor's House, Hyde Park Gate *173*
Charlecote Park, Warks. *14*, *24*, 59, 65, *84*, 85, *93*, 162–3
Charles I, King (1600–49) 82, *83*, 84
Charles II, King (1630–85) 86, 92
Chastleton House, Oxon. *8–9*
Chedworth Roman Villa, Gloucs. 62, *62*, *63*, 71
Chesterfield, Philip (Stanhope), 4th Earl of (1694–1773) 50
24 Cheyne Row, Chelsea *148*, 149, 150
Chinoiserie 115–16, *117*, 119
Chippendale, Thomas (1718–79) 116, *117*, *118*, 119, *119*, 127
    The Gentleman's & Cabinet Maker's Director 29, 119
Chippendale, Thomas, the Younger (1749–1822) 119, 141
Chirk Castle, Clwyd 155, *155*, 159
Chute, John (1701–76) 32, 104
Clandon Park, Surrey 100, *100*
Claremont, Surrey 20, 120, 140, 145, 146
Claydon House, Bucks. 15, 49, *49*, 107, *108*, 115, 116, 183
Clein, Franz (1582–1658) 82, *82*
Clive, Edward, 2nd Baron [later Earl of Powis] (1754–1839) 146
Clive, Robert, 1st Baron (1725–74) 20, 24, 146
Cliveden, Bucks. 89, 113, *113*, 159, 160
Clumber Park, Notts., Gothic Revival chapel 152, *153*
Cockerell, Charles Robert (1788–1863) 145
Colefax & Fowler 183
Coleshill, Oxon. 86
Coleton Fishacre, Devon 6, 17, 178–9, *179*
Committee of Taste 104
commodes *90*, 91, 110, *111*, 129
Composite order 19, *42*, *43*, 51, *51*
Condy, Nicholas (1799–1857) 31, 35
conservation movement 152
Corinthian order *42*, *43*, *48*, 49
Cotehele, Cornwall *34*, 35, 66, 68, 104, *104*
country house style 38
country houses, status of rooms affects decoration 19–20
Country Life 31
Crace, Edward (1725–99) 159
Crace, Frederick (1779–1859) 159
Crace, John (1754–1810) 159
Crace, John Dibblee (1839–1919) 13, 61, 133, 159

Crace, John Gregory (1809–89) 13, 155, 159
Cragside, Northumberland 31, 65, 161
Crane, Walter (1845–1915) 142, 150
Cressent, Charles (1685–1758) 110, *111*
Cromwell, Ralph, 3rd Lord (1394–1456) 18, *19*
Cure, Cornelius (d.1607) 81
Curzon, George, 1st Marquess (1859–1925) 147
Curzon, Sir Nathaniel, Bt (1726–1804) 15, 24, *127*

Dalyngrigge, Sir Edward (*c*. 1346–by 1395) 18
Danyers, Sir Thomas (*c*. 1294–1354) 35, 37
Dawkins-Pennant, George Hay (1764–1840) 145
de Morgan, William (1839–1917) 166, *166*
Delabrière, Louis André 129
Delany, Mary (neé Granville) (1700–88) 15
Delftware 92, *92*
doll's houses *10*, 29
Doric order *42*, 43, 44, *44*
Dormer, Sir Robert (d. 1552), tomb 66, 74
Dorn, Marion (1896–1964) *179*
Downhill, Co. Londonderry 133
D'Oyly Carte, Lady Dorothy *6*, 179
D'Oyly Carte, Rupert (1873–1948) 178, 179
Dryden, Edward (d. 1717) 68, 97, *97*
Dryden, Sir Erasmus (1553–1632) 78
Du Cerceau, Jacques Androuet (the Elder) (*c*. 1510–*c*. 1585) 52, 79
Duchess Street, London, Thomas Hope's house 140–1
Dufy, Raoul (1877–1953) *6*, 6, 179
Dungan, Richard 81
Dunham Massey, Cheshire 24, 86, *87*, 96, 97, 176
Dunster Castle, Somerset 52, 65
Dutton, Sir John, 2nd Bt (1684/5–1742/3) 98, *99*,
Dyck, Sir Anthony van (1599–1641) 82, *83*
Dyrham Park, Gloucs. 12–13, *22*, 23, 85, *92*, 95

East India Company 92, 116
Edgcumbe family, Cotehele 35, 104
Edward VII, King (1841–1910) 176
Edwardian style 176
Egerton, Wilbraham (1781–1856) 138
Egremont, George (Wyndham), 3rd Earl of (1751–1837) 136, 142–3
Egyptian Revival style 140–1
Elgin Marbles 130
Elizabeth I, Queen (1533–1603) 78, 162, 163
Elizabethan style 78–9
Etruscan style 134–5
Evelyn, John (1620–1706) 86, 89, 92

exhibitions 23

Fagan, Robert (1761–1816) 123
Farnborough Hall, Warks. 108, *108*
Favenza, Vincenzo 161
Felbrigg Hall, Norfolk 86, 89, *91*, 131
Fiorentino, Rosso (1494–1540) 65
Flaxman, John (1755–1826) 130–1, *131*
    'Shield of Achilles' 131, *131*
floral plasterwork *26*, 27, 86, *87*
Florence Court, Co. Fermanagh 108
Floris, Cornelis (1514–75) 27
Fonthill Abbey, Wilts. *14*, 104
Fowler, John (1906–77) *182*, 183, *183*

Garner, Thomas (1839–1906) 153
Gawthorpe Hall, Lancs. 27, *154*, 155
Gedde, Walter, *Booke of Sundry Draughtes* 81
George IV, King (1762–1830) 91, 98, 131, 136
Georgian era 98–9
Georgian Group 138
Gibbons, Grinling (1648–1721) 58, 66, *68*, 85, 86, *87*
Gibbs, James (1682–1754) 104
    A Book of Architecture 28, *28*
Gimson, Ernest (1864–1919) 165, 169
glaziers, Flemish *26*, 27
Godwin, Edward William (1833–86) 170–1
Goldfinger, Ernö (1902–87) 15, 180, *180*, *181*
Golle, Pierre *88*, 89
Goodrich Castle, Herefordshire 37
Gothic Revival 18, 20, 32, 104, 152–3, 154–5, 161
Gothick style *15*, *16*, 17, 18, 104
Goudge, Edward 86
Grand Tours 20, 24
The Grange, Fulham *169*
Great Coxwell Barn, Berks. 164
Great Exhibition (1851) 15, 146, 159, 166
Great Packington, Warks. 133
Greek Revival style 130–1
Green, Frank 37, *37*
Gresham, Sir Thomas (1519–79) 27
Greville, Mrs Ronald (1863–1942) 176
griffins *59*, 59
grotesque ornament 57, 61, *61*, 74, *75*
guilloche 62, *62*, *63*
Gwynne, Patrick (b. 1913) 180

Ham House, Surrey *43*, 43, 82, *82*, *83*, 86, 92, 115, 163
Hamilton, Sir William (1730–1803) 130, 134, *135*

Hampton Court Palace, Middx. 74, 89, 94
Hanbury Hall, Worcs. 85
Hardwick, Bess of *see* Shrewsbury, Elizabeth, Countess of
Hardwick Hall, Derbyshire 26, 27, 52, 65, 72–3, *78*, *78*, 79, *79*
Hardy, Thomas (1840–1928) 149
Hatchlands Park, Surrey 124
Hauduroy, Mark Anthony 13
Hayman, Francis (1708–76) 109
Heathcoat Amory family 156
Hegel, Georg (1770–1831) 11
heraldic ornament 52
heraldry 18
Herculaneum 61, 133, 134
Hinton Ampner, Hants. 138
Hoare, Sir Richard Colt (1758–1838) 119, 141
Hogarth, William (1697–1764) 99, *99*
Holbein, Hans (?1497–1543) 76, 77
Holland, Henry (1745–1806) 44, 68, 69, 120, 123, 136
Homewood, Esher, Surrey 180
Hope, Thomas (1769–1831) 130, 140–1
Hopper, Thomas (1776–1856) 145
Houghton Hall, Norfolk 20, 100
Houses of Parliament 152, 155, 159, 160
Howard, Henry, Earl of Surrey (1518–47) 57, 75
Hudson, Edward 31
Huguenot craftsmen 89, 94, 95

Ickworth, Suffolk 13, 61, 123, *132*, 133, 159
Ightham Mote, Kent 76, *77*, 178
Indian style 146–7
interiors, views of *30*, 31, 35
Ionic order 19, *42*, 43, 47, *47*, 54
Ionides, Basil (1884–1950) 179
Isaacson, Paul *61*, 68

Jacobean style 61, 65, 80–1
Jacobethan style 65, 162–3
Jensen, Gerrit [Johnson, Gerard] (active *c*. 1680–1715) 92
Jones, Inigo (1573–1652) 17, 82, 100, 103, 160
Joris, David 27

Kedleston Hall, Derbyshire 15, 120, 124, 127, *127*, 130, *130*, 133, 147, *147*
Kelmscott Manor, Oxon. 164
Kent, William (1685–1748) 100, *102*, 103
    Designs of Inigo Jones with some Additional Designs 28
Kéroualle, Louise de, Duchess of Portsmouth (1649–1734) 89
Killerton, Devon, Romanesque chapel 145
Kingston Lacy, Dorset 12, 56, 57, 62, *136*, 141, *141*, 160–1, *160*

Kipling, John Lockwood (1837–1911) 146, *146*
Kipling, Rudyard (1865–1936) 146–7, *146*
Knightshayes Court, Devon 20, 156, *157*, 159
Knole, Kent 26, 27, 43, 51, 57, 61, 65, *65*, 68, 75, 77, 80–1, *81*, *88*, 89

Lacock Abbey, Wilts. 31, 74, *75*, *82*, 104
Lafranchini brothers (*stuccadores*) 108
Laguerre, Louis (1663–1721) 85, 89
Lalique, René (1860–1945) *174*
Langley, Batty (1696–1751), *Gothic Architecture Improved* 104
Langlois, Pierre (active *c.* 1760) 129
Lanhydrock, Cornwall 66
Lanscroon, Gerard (*c.* 1655–1737) *85*
Lees-Milne, James (1908–97) 38
Legh, Thomas (1792–1857) 35, 131
Leoni, Giacomo (*c.* 1686–1746) 100, *100*
Leslie, Charles Robert (1794–1859) 142
Lethaby, William Richard (1857–1931) 161, 165, 166
Leyland, Frederick R. (1831–92) 173
Lichfield Cathedral 152
Liddell, Henry George (1811–98) 145
Lightfoot, Luke (*c.* 1722–89) 15, *106*, 108, 116
Lindisfarne Castle, Northumberland *30*, 31, 175
linenfold panelling 76, 77
Lock, Matthias (active *c.* 1724–69) *106*
Lockey, Rowland (*c.* 1565/7–1616) *76*
Lodge Park, Gloucs. 77, *102*, 103
Louis XIV, King of France (1638–1715) *88*, 89
Louis XIV style 89
Louis XV, King of France (1710–74) 110
Louis XV style 110, 113
Louis XVI, King of France (1754–93) 128, *128*, 129
Louis XVI style 128–9
Lucy, George (1714–86) 24
Lucy, George Hammond (1789–1845) 162
Lucy, Mary Elizabeth Hammond (neé Williams) (1803–90) 162
Lucy, Sir Thomas (before 1532–1600) 162, 163
Lutyens, Sir Edwin Landseer (1869–1944) 31, 145, 175
Lyme Park, Cheshire 27, 35, *35*, 37, 38, 43, 68, 138
Lyte, Henry 27
Lytes Cary, Somerset 77
Lyveden New Bield, Northants. 78

Mackintosh, Charles Rennie (1868–1928) 175
Macquoid, Percy (1852–1925) 176
Maiano, Giovanni da (1486/7–*c.* 1542/3) 74, *74*
marbled paper 13
marbling 13
Marot, Daniel (*c.* 1663–1752) 11, 92, 94–5

marquetry 90, *91*, 92, 93
Marshall, John (1765–1845) 141
Mary II, Queen (1662–94) 92, 115
Mary, Queen of Scots (1542–87) 78, *78*
May, Hugh (1621–84) 145
Mercier, Philippe (1689–1760) 106
Meyrick, Samuel Rush 37
Miller, Sanderson (1716–80) 104
Mills, William 145
Modern Movement 15, 154–5, 180
Mompesson House, Salisbury 97
Montacute, Somerset 51, *51*, 65, 77, 140
More, Sir Thomas (1478–1535) *76*, 77
Morris & Co. 164
Morris, William (1834–96) 11, 53, 152, 164–5, *165*, 166, 175
Mortlake tapestry factory 82
mosaics 62, *62*, 71
Mowl, Tim 145
Mulready, William (1786–1863) 142
murals 85, 89
Murray, William, 1st Earl of Dysart (*c.* 1600–55) 82

nabobs 20
Nash, John (1752–1835) 138, *139*, 152
Nash, Joseph (1808–78) 31
    Mansions of England in the Olden Time 37
Neo-classical designers 54, 58, 59, 61, 62, 66, 68, 71, 120
Neo-classical style 18, 119, 120, 123, 127
    Adam's version 124
Nicholls, Thomas 157
Norman Revival style 145
Nostell Priory, Yorks. 13, *29*, 76, 77, 108, 116, 117, *118*, 119, *119*, 123, 124

obelisks 140, 141
ormolu mounts 90, *91*, *91*
ornament prints 27, 28, 57
Orpen, Rebecca Dulcibella (1830–1923) *30*
Osterley Park, Middx. 20, 27, 52, 68, 84, 124, *125*, 134, *135*, 145
Oxborough church, Norfolk 74, *75*
Oxburgh Hall, Norfolk 78, *78*, 152, *153*, 159

Packwood House, Warks. 38, *38*
Pain, William (*c.* 1730–94?) 28–9
    The Builder's Pocket Treasure 29
    The Practical Builder 28, 29
Palladian style 10, 15, 16, *17*, 100, 103, 119, *119*, 124
Palladio, Andrea (1508–80) 82, 100
    Four Books of Architecture 17, 100
palmettes 47, 54, 55

Parker, William 23
Patch, Thomas (1725–82) 24, *24*
Pater, Walter (1838–94) 170
Patoun, William (d. 1783) 24
pattern-books 6, 7, 27, 28–9, 31
Peckover House, Cambs. 71
Penrhyn Castle, Gwynedd *144*, 145
period rooms 35, 37
Perret, Auguste (1874–1954) 180
Perritt, Thomas (1710–59) 108
Perritt, William (active *c.* 1724–70) 108, *108*, 109
Pether family *105*
Petworth, West Sussex 25, 68, 85, 90, *91*, 142–3, *143*
Pevsner, Sir Nikolaus (1902–83) 32
photography 31, 149
Pierce, Edward (*c.* 1635–95), the Younger 53, 67
Pierce, Edward (d. 1658), the Elder 28, 53
pietra dura 84, 85
Pineau, Nicolas (1684–1754) 110, 113, *113*, 143
Plas Newydd, Anglesey 89, 104
Polesden Lacey, Surrey 176, *177*
Pollen, John Hungerford (1820–1902) 37
Pompadour, Jeanne Antoinette Poisson, marquise de (1721–64) 110
Pompeian style 133
Pompeii 13, 61, 133, 134
porcelain 14, 92, 109, 115, 129
porches, internal 77
Portington, William 80, *81*
Powis Castle, Powys *1*, 24, 58, *58*, 60, 85, *85*, 89, *134*, 146, *162*, 163, *163*
Pratt, Sir Roger (1620–85) 12, 18–19, 86
Preston, John and Nathaniel 136, *137*
Pricke, Robert (active 1655–1700) 28
Pugin, A. W. N. (1812–52) 53, 149, 152, 154–5, *154*, *155*, 159
Pugin, Augustus Charles (*c.* 1769–1832) 154

Queen Anne style 97

Ranelagh Gardens, Chelsea 109
Raphael (Raffaello Sanzio) (1483–1520) 61, 91
Red House, Kent 164
Reformed Gothic style 152–3
Regency style 136, 138
Renaissance Revival 15, 57, 61, 65, 160–1
Renaissance style 18, 74–5
Repton, Humphry (1752–1818) 130, 138
Repton, John Adey (1775–1860) 130
Restoration style 86
Revett, Nicholas (1720–1804) 130

revivalism 32, *33*
Riesener, Jean-Henri (1734–1806) 128, *128*
Rievaulx Terrace, North Yorks. 103
Ripon, Henrietta, Marchioness of (d. 1907) 157
Ritson, Jonathan (d. 1846) 143
Robinson, Charles Henry (d. 1985) 178
Robinson, Sir Thomas (c. 1702–77) 108–9
Rococo designers 82, 113
Rococo Revival 58, 142–3
Rococo style 17, 58, 61, 89, 106–9, 119, 141
Rose, Joseph, the Elder (c. 1723–80) 108
Rothschild, James de (1878–1957) 179
roundels, terracotta 74, *74*
Royal Exchange, London 27
Rubens, Sir Peter Paul (1577–1640) 84
Ruskin, John (1819–1900) 11, 150, 164, 166, 170
Rysbrack, Michael (1694–1770) 99, *99*, 100

Sackville, Thomas, 1st Earl of Dorset (1536–1608) 80, 81
Saltram, Devon *2–3*, 15, *22*
Sandys, William 27
Sargent, John Singer (1856–1925) *176*
scagliola 12
Scott, Sir George Gilbert (1811–78) 161
Scott, Sir Walter (1771–1832) 37
Serlio, Sebastiano (1475–1554) 27, *50*
   The Five Books of Architecture 12, *12*, 27
Sèvres porcelain 129
Sezincote, Gloucs. 146
sgabello chairs 65, *82*
Shakespeare, William (1564–1616) 162
Sharington, Sir William (c. 1495–1553) 74, *75*
Shaw, Richard Norman (1831–1912) 161
Shaw's Corner, Herts. 175
Sheffield Park, East Sussex 104
Shrewsbury, Elizabeth, Countess of [Bess of Hardwick] (c. 1527–1608) 78
Shugborough, Staffs. 44, 130, *130*
Sizergh Castle, Cumbria 27, 37, 52, 77, 109
Smallhythe Place, Kent *149*, 171
Snowshill Manor, Gloucs. 169
social status 18–20, 23
Society for the Protection of Ancient Buildings 165
The Spectator 97
Speke Hall, Liverpool 173
Staffordshire figures *149*, 150
stained glass 26, 27, 32, 164
Standen, West Sussex 165, 166, *166*, *167*
state beds 85, 94–5, *95*
Steuart, George (c. 1730–1806) *120*, 123

Stoneacre, Kent 165, *169*
Stourhead, Wilts. 15, 100, 119, 141, 152
Stowe, Bucks. 31, 99, 104, 140, 141
strapwork 57, 58, 61, 65, *65*
Strawberry Hill, Twickenham 32, 104
Mr Straw's House, Worksop *140*, 141
Street, George Edmund (1824–81) 152–3, 166
Stuart, James 'Athenian' (1713–88) 54, 130, *130*, 133, 134
stuccadores 107–8
Studley Royal, North Yorks. 44
   St Mary's church 157
style defined 11
Sudbury Hall, Derbyshire 52, *53*, 58, 67, 86, 135, *182*, 183, *183*
sumptuary laws 18
Surrey, Henry (Howard), Earl of (1518–47) 57, 75
swags 47, 66, *66*, 79
Sykes, Sir Francis (1732–1804) 59

Tait, Robert Scott (active 1845–75) *148*, 149
Talbot, Henry Fox (1800–77) 31, *31*, 149
Talman, William (1650–1719) 85
tapestries 82, 146, 164
Tattershall Castle, Lincs. 18, *19*
Tatton Park, Cheshire 91, 138
Temple Mills, Leeds 141
Terry, Dame Ellen (1847–1928) 170, 171, *171*
Theatre Royal, Drury Lane 136
Thornhill, Sir James (1675–1734) 85
Tiffany, Louis (1848–1933) 175
Tijou, Jean (active 1689–1712) 89
Tintagel, Old Post Office 165
16 Tite Street, Chelsea 171, 173
Titus, Arch of 51
Tower of London 145
Treasurer's House, York *36*, 37
Trentham Hall, Staffs. 160
Tresham, Sir Thomas (1543?–1605) 78
Trevelyan, Sir Charles (1809–86) 146
Trevelyan, Pauline, Lady (1816–66) *150*
trophies 68, *68*
Tudor style 77
Tuscan order 19, *42*, 43, 50, *51*
typography 180

Uppark, West Sussex 21, 38, *39*, 55, *101*, 130, 183
   doll's house *10*
Upton House, Warks. 129, *178*, 179
Vallance, Aymer (1862–1943) 165, 175
Vanbrugh, Sir John (1664–1726) 97, 145
Vauxhall Gardens, London 109

Vernon, George (Venables-Vernon), 5th Lord (1803–66) 135
Verrio, Antonio (c. 1639–1707) 85
Versailles, Palace of *88*, 89, 91, 128, *128*
Victoria & Albert Museum 37
Victorian style 149–50
Villa Negroni, Rome 13, 133
Vitruvian scrolls 47, 71, *71*
Vitruvius Pollio, Marcus (active 46–30 BC) 18, 47, 49, 71
Vries, Hans Vredeman de (1527–1606) 27, 80
The Vyne, Hants. 27, *27*, *33*, 74, *74*, 77, *77*, 104

Waddesdon Manor, Bucks. 15, 89, 91, 110, *110*, 113, 128, 129, 142, 179
Wade, Charles Paget (1883–1956) 169
Wallington, Northumberland 108, 150, *150*
Walpole, Horace (1717–97), 4th Earl of Orford 32, 100, 103, 104, 120, 124, 134
Ward, Lady Anne (d. 1789) 15, 16, 17
Ward, Bernard [later 1st Viscount Bangor] (1719–81) 15, 16, 17
Warrington, 2nd Earl of *see* Booth, George
Webb, Philip Speakman (1831–1915) 164, 166, *167*, 169
Wedgwood, Josiah (1730–95) *22*, 23, 134–5
Weekes, Fred 157
West Wycombe, Bucks. 129, 130
Whistler, James Abbott McNeill (1834–1903) 173
Whistler, Rex (1905–44) 58, 104, *142*, 143
Wightwick Manor, Wolverhampton 164–5, *165*
Wilde, Oscar (1854–1900) 170, 171, 173
Willcox, J. M. 163
Willement, Thomas (1786–1871) 145, 162–3
William III, King (1650–1702) 92, 94
William and Mary style 92
2 Willow Road, Hampstead 15, 180, *180*, *181*
Wilson, Sir William (1641–1710) 58
Wilton House, Wilts. 103
Wimpole Hall, Cambs. 104, 134
Windsor Castle, Berks. 145
Winn, Sir Rowland, 5th Bt (1739–85) 119
Wolsey, Thomas, Cardinal (?1472–1530) 74
Woolner, Thomas (1825–92) 150
Wyatt, Benjamin Dean (1775–c.1855) 142
Wyatt, James (1746–1813) 44, 104, 120, *121*, 152
Wyatt, Lewis (1777–1853) 35, 138
Wyatt, Richard James (1795–1850) 123
Wyatt, Samuel (1737–1807) 44, 120
Wyatville, Sir Jeffry (1766–1840) 145

Picture Credits

British Architectural Library, RIBA, London: p.12; p.153. British Museum, London: p.23; p.99. *Country Life* Picture Library: p.6; p.19; p.30 (left); p.39; p.75 (left); p.108. Christie's Images: p.7. Conway Library, Courtauld Institute of Art: p.98 (left); Courtesy of the Fox Talbot Museum, Lacock, Wiltshire: p.31. © Estate of Rex Whistler 2002. All Rights Reserved, DACS: p.142. London Library: p.28; p.42. National Trust: p.82 (right); p.83; p.113; p.130; p.152; p.170. National Trust/Brenda Norrish: pp.96/97. NTPL: p.51 (left); pp.64/65; pp.94/95; p.95 (right); p.121; p.155 (right). NTPL/Matthew Antrobus: p.16; p.17. NTPL/Bill Batten: p.20; p.36; p.86 (right); p.125; p.135. NTPL/John Bethell: p.78 (bottom). NTPL/P.A.Burton: p.79. NTPL/Michael Caldwell: p.144 (left and right); p.167. NTPL/Andreas von Einsiedel: pp.2/3; p.13; pp.14/15; p.18; p.21; p.22 (left and right); p.25; p.26 (left); p.29; p.34; p.35; p.38; pp.40/41; p.48; p.49; p.50; p.51 (bottom); p.61; p.65 (right); p.67; p.68; p.75 (right); pp.80/81; p.82 (left); p.85; p.88 (left and right); p.90; p.92; p.97 (right); p.98 (right); p.101; p.103; p.104; p.107; p.112; pp.114/115; p.117; p.118; p.132; p.143; p.151; p.157; pp.164/165; p.165 (right); pp.168/169; p.177; p.178; p.182; p.183. NTPL/Mark Fiennes: pp.54/55; p.66; pp.70/71; p.78 (top). NTPL/Roy Fox: p.166; pp.172/173. NTPL/Geoffrey Frosh: p.55 (right). NTPL/Jonathon Gibson: p.119. NTPL/Dennis Gilbert: p.174 (left). NTPL/John Hammond: endpapers; p.1; p.26 (right); p.46; p.57 (left and right); p.58; p.60; p.69; pp.72/73; p.76 (left); p.105; p.109; p.120; pp.126/127; p.131; p.134; p.140; p.146; p.147 (left); p.149; p.155 (left); p.156; p.158; p.162; p.163; p.169 (right); p.171; p.174 (right); p.176; p.179 (left and right); p.180. NTPL/Philip Harris: p.181. NTPL/Angelo Hornak: p.139. NTPL/Tymn Lintell: p.150. NTPL/Nadia Mackenzie: p.10; p.47; p.76 (right); p.81 (right); p.86 (left); p.91 (left); p.100; p.102; p.123; p.147 (right); p.159. NTPL/Rob Matheson: p.148. NTPL/James Mortimer: p.33; p.74; p.77; p.122; p.129; p.136; p.141; p.160 (left); pp.160/161. NTPL/Richard Pink: p.56. NTPL/Patrick Prendergast: pp.44/45; p.137. NTPL/Ian Shaw: pp.8/9; p.62; p.63. NTPL/Mike Williams: p.87; p.154. NTPL/Derrick E. Witty: p.24 (left and right); p.27; p.30 (right); p.59; p.84; p.93. National Trust, Waddesdon Manor (Hugo Maertens): p.91 (right); p.111; p.128. John Paul Photography /courtesy of Mr and Mrs Grant of Rothiemurchus: p.43. Rijksmuseum-Stichting, Amsterdam: pp.52/53. Victoria and Albert Museum, London: p.106. Waldorf Astoria Hotel, New York: p.37.

NTPL: National Trust Photo Library

Acknowledgements

This book grows out of many years working on the National Trust's guidebooks. To all those, too numerous to name, both inside and outside the Trust, who have helped me produce these guides, I am immensely grateful. But I must mention in particular my past and present assistants, Julia Muir and Helen Dunkerley, who have cheerfully shouldered much of the burden. Margaret Willes and Tim Knox kindly and critically commented on an early draft. Barbara Mercer has patiently edited an editor, and Sarah Mattinson has found a style for style. This book also owes a huge debt to Maggie Gowan and her team in the National Trust Photographic Library, who have commissioned almost every image in it and put up with my constant demands for yet more photographs.

And last, and most, I want to thank Molly, who has grown up with this book, and Jenny, who has helped in many, many ways with it – and despite it. It is for them.

Oliver Garnett